The
Darlings
of
Mendon,
Massachusetts

Susan Salisbury

HERITAGE BOOKS
2020

HERITAGE BOOKS

AN IMPRINT OF HERITAGE BOOKS, INC.

Books, CDs, and more—Worldwide

For our listing of thousands of titles see our website
at
www.HeritageBooks.com

Published 2020 by
HERITAGE BOOKS, INC.
Publishing Division
5810 Ruatan Street
Berwyn Heights, Md. 20740

Heritage Books by the author:
Descendants of Walter Cook
My Family: Lariviere-Morin
Southern Massachusetts Cemetery Collection: Volumes 1 and 2
The Darlings of Mendon, Massachusetts
The Thayers of Mendon, Massachusetts
The Wheelocks of Mendon, Massachusetts

International Standard Book Number
Paperbound: 978-0-7884-2351-2

Descendants of Denice Darling

1. Denice² Darling (George¹) was born 1640 in England, and died 25 January 1716/17 in Mendon, Massachusetts. He married **Hannah Frances** 03 November 1663 in Braintree, Massachusetts, daughter of John Frances and Rose Deacon. She was born 1650 in Braintree, Massachusetts, and died 17 September 1688.

Notes for Denice Darling:
Dennis and his family moved to Mendon, Massachusetts around 1677

Children of Denice Darling and Hannah Frances are:

2	i.	Cornelius Darling, born 04 January 1662/63 in Braintree, Massachusetts; died 11 May 1663 in Braintree, Massachusetts.
+ 3	ii.	Captain John Darling, born 02 September 1664 in Braintree, Massachusetts; died 29 May 1753 in Bellingham, Massachusetts.
4	iii.	Aaron Darling, born 18 June 1667 in Braintree, Massachusetts; died 18 June 1667 in Braintree, Massachusetts.
+ 5	iv.	Sarah Darling, born 26 January 1668/69 in Braintree, Massachusetts; died 12 October 1703 in Mendon, Massachusetts.
+ 6	v.	Cornelius Darling, born 25 January 1674/75 in Braintree, Massachusetts; died in Bellingham, Massachusetts.
+ 7	vi.	Hannah Darling, born 14 June 1677 in Braintree, Massachusetts.
8	vii.	Ebenezer Darling, born 08 January 1678/79 in Mendon, Massachusetts. He married Mary Wheaton 03 March 1697/98 in Rehoboth, Massachusetts.
+ 9	viii.	Daniel Darling, born 28 April 1682 in Mendon, Massachusetts; died 03 February 1744/45 in Mendon, Massachusetts.
+ 10	ix.	Elizabeth Darling, born 02 July 1685 in Mendon, Massachusetts.

+   11   x.   Benjamin Darling, born 11 February 1686/87 in Mendon,
               Massachusetts; died 18 May 1772 in Millville,
               Massachusetts.

Generation No. 2

3. Captain John[3] Darling (Denice[2], George[1]) was born 02
September 1664 in Braintree, Massachusetts, and died 29 May
1753 in Bellingham, Massachusetts. He married **(1) Elizabeth
Thompson** 20 January 1685/86 in Mendon, Massachusetts,
daughter of John Thompson and Thankful Woodland. She was
born 28 June 1671 in Braintree, Massachusetts, and died 03 April
1687 in Mendon, Massachusetts. He married **(2) Elizabeth
Morse** 1691 in Mendon, Massachusetts, daughter of Samuel
Morse. She was born 08 February 1665/66, and died 1718. He
married **(3) Anne Rockwood** 02 January 1687/88 in Boston,
Massachusetts, daughter of John Rockwood and Joanna Ford. She
was born 25 August 1669 in Mendon, Massachusetts, and died 30
April 1690 in Mendon, Massachusetts.

Children of Captain Darling and Elizabeth Thompson are:

+   12   i.   John[4] Darling, born 01 April 1687 in Mendon,
               Massachusetts; died 11 June 1760 in Millville,
               Massachusetts.
     13   ii.   Seth Darling, died 30 October 1798 in Mendon,
               Massachusetts.
     14   iii. Pardon Darling, died 20 October 1799 in Mendon,
               Massachusetts.
+   15   iv.   Abigail Darling, born 14 July 1708 in Mendon,
               Massachusetts; died 1744.

Children of Captain Darling and Elizabeth Morse are:

+   16   i.   Ruth[4] Darling, born 20 September 1695 in Mendon,
               Massachusetts; died 1729 in Mendon, Massachusetts.
+   17   ii.   Captain Samuel Darling, born 18 March 1692/93; died 17
               February 1774.
     18   iii. Elizabeth Darling.
     19   iv.   Hannah Darling.
     20   v.   Mary Darling

	21	vi.	Abigail Darling
	22	vii.	Deborah Darling, born 08 January 1713/14 in Mendon, Massachusetts; died in Bellingham, Massachusetts. She married Henry Bosworth 25 April 1732 in Smithfield, Rhode Island; born 1711.
+	23	viii.	Ebenezer Darling, born 02 March 1701/02 in Mendon, Massachusetts; died 22 September 1750 in Cumberland, Rhode Island.
+	24	ix.	Margaret Darling, born 19 August 1700 in Mendon, Massachusetts.
+	25	x.	Martha Darling, born 10 March 1705/06 in Mendon, Massachusetts; died January 1783 in Bellingham, Massachusetts.
+	26	xi.	Ruth Darling, born 20 September 1695 in Mendon, Massachusetts; died 1727 in Mendon, Massachusetts.
+	27	xii.	Elizabeth Darling, born 03 January 1691/92 in Mendon, Massachusetts; died 15 June 1760 in Millville, Massachusetts.
+	28	xiii.	Samuel Darling, born 18 March 1692/93 in Mendon, Massachusetts; died 17 February 1774 in Bellingham, Massachusetts.
+	29	xiv.	Hannah Darling, born 01 November 1697 in Mendon, Massachusetts; died 20 May 1761 in Bellingham, Massachusetts.
+	30	xv.	Mary Darling, born 22 May 1704 in Mendon, Massachusetts.
+	31	xvi.	Abigail Darling, born 14 July 1708 in Mendon, Massachusetts; died 1744.
	32	xvii.	Rachel Darling, born 14 May 1711 in Mendon, Massachusetts.
+	33	xviii.	Deborah Darling, born 08 January 1712/13 in Mendon, Massachusetts; died 17 March 1749/50 in New Jersey.

Child of Captain Darling and Anne Rockwood is:

+	34	i.	Anna[4] Darling, born 20 April 1689 in Mendon, Massachusetts; died 02 January 1753 in Rehoboth, Massachusetts.

5. Sarah[3] Darling (Denice[2], George[1]) was born 26 January 1668/69 in Braintree, Massachusetts, and died 12 October 1703 in Mendon, Massachusetts. She married **(1) Jonathan Thayer**, son of Ferdinando Thayer and Huldah Hayward. He was born 18

March 1658/59 in Braintree, Massachusetts, and died 1691 in Mendon, Massachusetts. She married **(2) John Wilson** 1694.

Child of Sarah Darlingand Jonathan Thayer is:

35   i.   Hezekiah[4] Thayer, born 08 February 1686/87 in Mendon, Massachusetts; died 13 January 1688/89 in Mendon, Massachusetts.

Child of Sarah Darling and John Wilson is:

36   i.   John[4] Wilson, born 1695 in Mendon, Massachusetts.

    6. Cornelius[3] Darling (Denice[2], George[1]) was born 25 January 1674/75 in Braintree, Massachusetts, and died in Bellingham, Massachusetts. He married **(1) Mary Frebray** 1694 in Mendon, Massachusetts, daughter of Richard Frebary. She was born 1675 in Mendon, Massachusetts. He married **(2) Sarah Mitchell** 1720 in Mendon, Massachusetts, daughter of John Mitchell and Hannah Spofford.

Children of Cornelius Darling and Mary Frebray are:

37   i.   Mary[4] Darling, born 13 December 1695 in Mendon, Massachusetts.

+   38   ii.   David Darling, born 1697 in Attleboro, Massachusetts; died 02 June 1751 in Bellingham, Massachusetts.

+   39   iii.   Cornelius Darling, born 14 June 1698 in Mendon, Massachusetts; died 17 February 1783 in Bellingham, Massachusetts.

+   40   iv.   Richard Darling, born 09 December 1700 in Rehoboth, Massachusetts.

41   v.   Sarah Darling, born 14 March 1701/02 in Rehoboth, Massachusetts.

42   vi.   John Darling, born 17 August 1705 in Rehoboth, Massachusetts. He married Sarah Mitchell.

Child of Cornelius Darling and Sarah Mitchell is:

+   43   i.   Jane[4] Darling, born 17 December 1721 in Bellingham, Massachusetts.

7. Hannah[3] Darling (Denice[2], George[1]) was born 14 June 1677 in Braintree, Massachusetts. She married **John Martin** 25 December 1701 in Rehoboth, Massachusetts.

Children of Hannah Darling and John Martin are:
+ 44   i.   John[4] Martin, born 14 May 1703.
   45   ii.   Mary Martin, born 03 January 1704/05.
   46   iii.   Thomas Martin, born 18 August 1706.

9. Daniel[3] Darling (Denice[2], George[1]) was born 28 April 1682 in Mendon, Massachusetts, and died 03 February 1744/45 in Mendon, Massachusetts. He married **Lydia Cook** 1705 in Mendon, Massachusetts, daughter of Samuel Cook and Lydia White. She was born 1685 in Mendon, Massachusetts.

Children of Daniel Darling and Lydia Cook are:
+ 47   i.   Abigail[4] Darling, born 11 October 1706 in Mendon, Massachusetts; died 1747 in Mendon, Massachusetts.
+ 48   ii.   Daniel Darling, born 28 March 1709 in Mendon, Massachusetts; died May 1778 in Mendon, Massachusetts.
+ 49   iii.   Lydia Darling, born 05 January 1710/11 in Mendon, Massachusetts.
+ 50   iv.   Samuel Darling, born 18 March 1713/14 in Mendon, Massachusetts; died 1795 in Mendon, Massachusetts.
+ 51   v.   Susannah Darling, born 02 August 1717 in Mendon, Massachusetts; died 1778 in Douglas, Massachusetts.
+ 52   vi.   Kezia Darling, born 30 November 1719 in Mendon, Massachusetts; died 1801.
   53   vii.   Peter Darling, born 12 August 1722 in Mendon, Massachusetts; died 31 January 1797 in Mendon, Massachusetts. He married Sarah Thompson 1747; born 1726.
+ 54   viii.   William Darling, born 15 January 1729/30 in Mendon, Massachusetts; died 26 July 1819 in Sutton, Massachusetts.
   55   ix.   Abner Darling, born 07 March 1732/33 in Mendon, Massachusetts.

10. Elizabeth[3] Darling (Denice[2], George[1]) was born 02 July 1685 in Mendon, Massachusetts. She married **Obadiah Wheelock** 08 January 1707/08 in Mendon, Massachusetts, son of

Benjamin Wheelock and Elizabeth French. He was born 21 April 1685 in Medfield, Massachusetts.

Children of Elizabeth Darling and Obadiah Wheelock are:

56	i.	Ebenezer[4] Wheelock, born 30 August 1718 in Mendon, Massachusetts. He married Mary Slocum.
57	ii.	Margaret Wheelock born 18 February 1722/23 in Mendon, Massachusetts. She married James Albee 16 July 1739 in Mendon, Massachusetts
+ 58	iii.	Obadiah Wheelock, born 21 September 1712 in Mendon, Massachusetts.
59	iv.	Rebecca Wheelock, born 30 August 1720 in Mendon, Massachusetts She married Benjamin Fiske 16 November 1747 in Mendon, Massachusetts; born 07 May 1724.
60	v.	Elizabeth Wheelock, born 11 January 1708/09 in Mendon, Massachusetts. She married (1) Ephraim Daniels 03 July 1733 in Mendon, Massachusetts. She married (2) John Rockwood 18 March 1750/51 in Mendon, Massachusetts; born 22 August 1696 in Mendon, Massachusetts.
61	vi.	Hannah Wheelock, born 18 August 1716 in Mendon, Massachusetts She married Joshua Underwood 16 February 1736/37 in Mendon, Massachusetts.
+ 62	vii.	Josiah Wheelock, born 30 March 1725 in Mendon, Massachusetts; died 28 December 1794 in Milford, Massachusetts.
+ 63	viii.	Samuel Wheelock, born 06 September 1714 in Mendon, Massachusetts.
64	ix.	Ebenezer Wheelock, born 30 August 1718 in Mendon, Massachusetts; died 06 May 1801 in Bellingham, Massachusetts. He married Mary Sleeman.
65	x.	Margaret Wheelock, born 18 February 1722/23 in Mendon, Massachusetts. She married James Albee.

11. Benjamin[3] Darling (Denice[2], George[1]) was born 11 February 1686/87 in Mendon, Massachusetts, and died 18 May 1772 in Millville, Massachusetts. He married **(1) Mehitable White** 11 June 1708 in Mendon, Massachusetts, daughter of Thomas White and Mehitable Thornton. She was born 22 January 1688/89 in Mendon, Massachusetts, and died 1730 in Mendon, Massachusetts. He married **(2) Susanna Benson** 17 April 1760 in Mendon, Massachusetts, daughter of Benoni Benson and Sarah Thayer.

Notes for Benjamin Darling:
Benjamin was a boat builder.....Benjamin Darling was buried on
20 May 1772, at the Chestnut Hill Meeting House Cemetery,
located on Chestnut Hill Road in Millville, Massachusetts

Notes for Mehitable White:
Mehitable White is also buried at the Chestnut Hill Meeting House
Cemetery, located on Chestnut Hill Road in Millville,
Massachusetts

Children of Benjamin Darling and Mehitable White are:

	66	i.	Mehitable[4] Darling, born 10 November 1709 in Mendon, Massachusetts. She married Joseph How 12 April 1770.
+	67	ii.	Deborah Darling, born 22 April 1711 in Mendon, Massachusetts.
+	68	iii.	Benjamin Darling, born 15 March 1713/14 in Mendon, Massachusetts.
+	69	iv.	Joseph Darling, born 21 April 1716 in Mendon, Massachusetts; died 1787 in Mendon, Massachusetts.
+	70	v.	Ebenezer Darling, born 25 August 1718 in Mendon, Massachusetts; died 25 November 1806 in Glocester, Rhode Island.
+	71	vi.	Peter Darling, born 12 June 1720 in Mendon, Massachusetts; died 16 May 1818 in Cumberland, Rhode Island.
+	72	vii.	Hannah Darling, born 25 March 1722 in Mendon, Massachusetts; died 07 February 1799 in Mendon, Massachusetts.
+	73	viii.	Abigail Darling, born 15 March 1723/24 in Mendon, Massachusetts; died 03 August 1809 in Burrillville, Rhode Island.
+	74	ix.	Samuel Darling, born 01 August 1726 in Mendon, Massachusetts; died 1763 in Millville, Massachusetts.
+	75	x.	Elizabeth Darling, born 11 April 1729 in Mendon, Massachusetts; died 23 March 1778 in Mendon, Massachusetts.
+	76	xi.	Thomas Darling, born 07 May 1730 in Mendon, Massachusetts; died 22 October 1776 in Mendon, Massachusetts.
+	77	xii.	Deborah Darling, born 22 April 1711 in Mendon, Massachusetts.

Child of Benjamin Darling and Susanna Benson is:
+   78   i.   Anna[4] Darling, born 22 June 1761 in Mendon,
                 Massachusetts.

Generation No. 3

12. John[4] Darling (Captain John[3], Denice[2], George[1]) was
born 01 April 1687 in Mendon, Massachusetts, and died 11 June
1760 in Millville, Massachusetts. He married **(1) Hannah Staples**
05 January 1707/08 in Mendon, Massachusetts, daughter of
Abraham Staples and Mary Randall. She was born 13 May 1686
in Mendon, Massachusetts. He married **(2) Margaret Webb** 23
February 1746/47 in Smithfield, Rhode Island, daughter of Daniel
Webb and Mary Beckett.

Children of John Darling and Hannah Staples are:
     79   i.   Hannah[5] Darling, born 26 May 1710 in Mendon,
                  Massachusetts.
+   80   ii. Mary Darling, born 02 March 1711/12.
+   81   iii. Elizabeth Darling, born 07 November 1712 in Mendon,
                  Massachusetts.
+   82   iv. John Darling, born 01 December 1717 in Mendon,
                  Massachusetts; died 24 August 1798 in Cumberland, Rhode
                  Island.
+   83   v.   Pelatiah Darling, born 28 February 1719/20 in Mendon,
                  Massachusetts; died 30 June 1796 in Mendon,
                  Massachusetts.
     84   vi. Margaret Darling, born 12 January 1721/22 in Mendon,
                  Massachusetts. She married Jacob Mowry.
+   85   vii. Ruth Darling, born 01 July 1726 in Mendon, Massachusetts.

15. Abigail[4] Darling (Captain John[3], Denice[2], George[1]) was
born 14 July 1708 in Mendon, Massachusetts, and died 1744. She
married **John Thayer** 27 July 1727 in Mendon, Massachusetts son
of Isaac Thayer and Hannah Winter. He was born 06 May 1706 in
Mendon, Massachusetts'

Child of Abigail Darling and John Thayer is:
+   86   i.   Abigail[5] Thayer, born 1730 in Mendon, Massachusetts; died
                  1790.

16. Ruth[4] Darling (Captain John[3], Denice[2], George[1]), was born 20 September 1695 in Mendon, Massachusetts, and died 1729 in Mendon, Massachusetts. She married **Thomas Thayer** 05 January 1714/15 in Mendon, Massachusetts, son of Thomas Thayer and Mary Pool. He was born 14 January 1694/95 in Mendon, Massachusetts, and died 01 May 1738 in Mendon, Massachusetts.

Children of Ruth Darling and Thomas Thayer are:

87		i.	Thomas[5] Thayer born 23 January 1719/20 in Mendon, Massachusetts He married Susannah Blake 15 December 1751 in Smithfield, Rhode Island.
+	88	ii.	Elizabeth Thayer, born 17 February 1723/24 in Uxbridge, Massachusetts; died 27 August 1797 in Uxbridge, Massachusetts.

17. Captain Samuel[4] Darling (Captain John[3], Denice[2], George[1]) was born 18 March 1692/93, and died 17 February 1774. He married **Mary Thompson** 15 December 1716, daughter of John Thompson and Hannah Wight. She was born 11 March 1693/94 in Mendon, Massachusetts, and died 07 June 1740 in Bellingham, Massachusetts.

Children of Captain Darling and Mary Thompson are:

+	89	i.	Deacon Samuel[5] Darling, born 19 January 1718/19; died 12 June 1814.
	90	ii.	Elizabeth Darling.
	91	iii.	Ruth Darling
	92	iv.	Abigail Darling.
	93	v.	John Darling.
	94	vi.	Rachel Darling.
	95	vii.	Penelope Darling.

23. Ebenezer[4] Darling (Captain John[3], Denice[2], George[1]) was born 02 March 1701/02 in Mendon, Massachusetts, and died 22 September 1750 in Cumberland, Rhode Island. He married **Abial** 1721.

Children of Ebenezer Darling and Abial are:
+ 96   i.   Joseph[5] Darling, born 29 July 1722 in Bellingham, Massachusetts.
  97   ii. Esther Darling, born 28 May 1724 in Bellingham, Massachusetts.
+ 98   iii. Timothy Darling, born 30 January 1725/26 in Bellingham, Massachusetts.
  99   iv. John Darling, born 29 April 1733 in Bellingham, Massachusetts. He married Anna Jillson 1755 in Cumberland, Rhode Island; born 14 October 1736 in Cumberland, Rhode Island.
  100   v.   Mary Darling, born 1733 in Cumberland, Rhode Island; died 02 August 1771.
  101   vi. Abial Darling, born 1740 in Cumberland, Rhode Island. She married John Marble 07 August 1760 in Cumberland, Rhode Island.
  102   vii. Rachel Darling, born 1743 in Cumberland, Rhode Island. She married Daniel Trask 29 August 1765 in Smithfield, Rhode Island.

24. Margaret[4] Darling (Captain John[3], Denice[2], George[1]) was born 19 August 1700 in Mendon, Massachusetts. She married **John French** 1722 in Bellingham, Massachusetts, son of John French and Experience Thayer. He was born 16 April 1699 in Braintree, Massachusetts.

Children of Margaret Darling and John French are:
  103   i.   Jesse French, born 09 October 1723 in Mendon, Massachusetts.
  104   ii. Jonah French, born in Mendon, Massachusetts.
  105   iii. John French, born 14 March 1727/28 in Mendon, Massachusetts.
  106   iv. Margaret French, born 10 June 1729 in Mendon, Massachusetts.
  107   v.   Anna French, born 25 August 1733 in Mendon, Massachusetts.
  108   vi. Hannah French, born 25 August 1733 in Mendon, Massachusetts.
  109   vii. William French, born 28 May 1737 in Mendon, Massachusetts.

25. Martha[4] Darling (Captain John[3], Denice[2], George[1]) was born 10 March 1705/06 in Mendon, Massachusetts, and died January 1783 in Bellingham, Massachusetts. She married **Benjamin Thompson** 10 March 1725/26 in Bellingham, Massachusetts, son of John Thompson and Hannah Wight.

Children of Martha Darling and Benjamin Thompson are:

110	i.	Benoni[5] Thompson, born 10 May 1727.
111	ii.	Tamar Thompson, born 10 March 1727/28.
112	iii.	Martha Thompson, born 05 March 1728/29 in Bellingham, Massachusetts. She married (1) Samuel Buxton; died 15 June 1777. She married (2) Seth Hall 22 April 1757 in Bellingham, Massachusetts.
113	iv.	Mary Thompson, born 05 March 1728/29 in Bellingham, Massachusetts. She married Samuel Wight 18 October 1752.
114	v.	Benjamin Thompson, born 09 May 1731 in Bellingham, Massachusetts.
115	vi.	Samuel Thompson, born 20 July 1733 in Bellingham, Massachusetts. He married Rhoda Smith 16 July 1761 in Smithfield, Rhode Island.
116	vii.	Timothy Thompson, born 15 May 1735 in Bellingham, Massachusetts.
117	viii.	Elizabeth Thompson, born 03 August 1737 in Bellingham, Massachusetts.
118	ix.	Joanna Thompson, born 03 August 1739 in Smithfield, Rhode Island.
119	x.	John Thompson, born 06 June 1741 in Smithfield, Rhode Island.
120	xi.	Roger Thompson, born 31 December 1744 in Smithfield, Rhode Island.
121	xii.	Ebenezer Thompson, born 27 October 1751 in Smithfield, Rhode Island. He married Sarah Applin.

26. Ruth[4] Darling (Captain John[3], Denice[2], George[1]) was born 20 September 1695 in Mendon, Massachusetts, and died 1727 in Mendon, Massachusetts. She married **Thomas Thayer** 05 July 1715 in Mendon, Massachusetts, son of Thomas Thayer and Mary Pool.

Children of Ruth Darling and Thomas Thayer are:

+	122	i.	Priscilla⁵ Thayer, born 06 June 1717 in Mendon, Massachusetts.
+	123	ii.	Peter Thayer, born 16 April 1720 in Mendon, Massachusetts.
	124	iii.	Thomas Thayer, born 23 January 1720/21.
	125	iv.	Elizabeth Thayer, born 13 February 1723/24 in Uxbridge, Massachusetts.
	126	v.	Patience Thayer, born 1726 in Mendon, Massachusetts; died 24 February 1812. She married John Legg 03 May 1747 in Mendon, Massachusetts.

27. Elizabeth⁴ Darling (Captain John³, Denice², George¹) was born 03 January 1691/9? in Mendon, Massachusetts, and died 15 June 1760 in Millville, Massachusetts. She married **Joseph Brown** 1718, son of John Brown and Anna Mason. He was born 19 May 1690 in Swansea, Massachusetts, and died 1762 in Taunton, Massachusetts.

Children of Elizabeth Darling and Joseph Brown are:

	127	i.	Caleb Brown, born 30 June 1720.
	128	ii.	Joshua Brown, born 14 May 1722.
	129	iii.	Joseph Brown, born 04 September 1724.
	130	iv.	Levi Brown, born 1727.
	131	v.	William Brown, born 1730.

28. Samuel⁴ Darling (Captain John³, Denice², George¹) was born 18 March 1692/93 in Mendon, Massachusetts, and died 17 February 1774 in Bellingham, Massachusetts. He married **(1) Mary Thompson** 05 December 1716 in Mendon, Massachusetts, daughter of John Thompson and Hannah Wight. She was born 11 March 1693/94 in Mendon, Massachusetts, and died 07 June 1740 in Bellingham, Massachusetts. He married **(2) Penelope Butterworth** 12 September 1741 in Bellingham, Massachusetts. She was born 1697. He married **(3) Thomasin Adams** 07 February 1760, daughter of Jonathan Adams and Thomasin Sheffield. She was born 21 August 1699 in Medway, Massachusetts.

Children of Samuel Darling and Mary Thompson are:

+	132	i.	Samuel[5] Darling, born 09 January 1718/19 in Bellingham, Massachusetts; died 12 June 1814 in Bellingham, Massachusetts.
+	133	ii.	Michael Darling, born 06 March 1722/23 in Bellingham, Massachusetts; died 25 February 1803 in Ballston, New York.
+	134	iii.	Elizabeth Darling, born 31 August 1725 in Bellingham, Massachusetts; died 09 May 1809 in Medway, Massachusetts.
+	135	iv.	Ruth Darling, born 03 July 1728 in Bellingham, Massachusetts.
+	136	v.	Abigail Darling, born 16 February 1730/31 in Bellingham, Massachusetts; died 23 June 1826 in Bellingham, Massachusetts.
+	137	vi.	John Darling, born 29 April 1733 in Bellingham, Massachusetts; died 02 February 1800 in Bellingham, Massachusetts.
	138	vii.	Rachel Darling, born 11 June 1735 in Bellingham, Massachusetts; died 1820 in Bellingham, Massachusetts.
	139	viii.	Jerusha Darling, born 02 November 1737 in Bellingham, Massachusetts.
+	140	ix.	Joshua Darling, born 20 November 1739 in Bellingham, Massachusetts; died 21 May 1815 in Bellingham, Massachusetts.

Child of Samuel Darling and Penelope Butterworth is:

| + | 141 | i. | Penelope[5] Darling, born 25 August 1742 in Bellingham, Massachusetts. |

29. Hannah[4] Darling (Captain John[3], Denice[2], George[1]) was born 01 November 1697 in Mendon, Massachusetts, and died 20 May 1761 in Bellingham, Massachusetts. She married **Samuel Thompson** 05 January 1724/25 in Bellingham, Massachusetts, son of John Thompson and Hannah Wight. He was born 02 July 1696 in Mendon, Massachusetts.

Children of Hannah Darling and Samuel Thompson are:

| | 142 | i. | Gideon Thompson, born 1730 in Mendon, Massachusetts. He married Anna West 1804. |
| | 143 | ii. | Samuel Thompson, born 1735 in Mendon, Massachusetts. He married Grace Baker Rogers 1767. |

144   iii.   Hannah Thompson, born 12 June 1735 in Mendon, Massachusetts. She married Thomas Holland 13 February 1764; born 20 October 1737 in Boston, Massachusetts.

30. Mary⁴ Darling (Captain John³, Denice², George¹) was born 22 May 1704 in Mendon, Massachusetts. She married **Jonathan Draper** 29 October 1729 in Bellingham, Massachusetts, son of Jonathan Draper and Sarah Jackson. He was born 29 October 1703.

Children of Mary Darling and Jonathan Draper are:

+ 145   i.   Jonathan Draper, born 10 May 1730 in Bellingham, Massachusetts.
146   ii.   Mary Draper, born 11 May 1735 in Bellingham, Massachusetts.
147   iii.   Rachel Draper, born 14 March 1738/39 in Bellingham, Massachusetts.

31. Abigail⁴ Darling (Captain John³, Denice², George¹) was born 14 July 1708 in Mendon, Massachusetts, and died 1744. She married **(1) Nathaniel Chickering** 20 February 1725/26 in Wrentham, Massachusetts, son of Nathaniel Chickering and Mary Throp. She married **(2) John Thayer** 27 July 1727, son of Isaac Thayer and Mary.

Child of Abigail Darling and Nathaniel Chickering is:

148   i.   Nathaniel Chickering, born 02 December 1728 in Wrentham, Massachusetts.

33. Deborah⁴ Darling (Captain John³, Denice², George¹) was born 08 January 1712/13 in Mendon, Massachusetts, and died 17 March 1749/50 in New Jersey. She married **Henry Bosworth** 25 April 1732 in Smithfield, Rhode Island, son of Ichabod Bosworth and Sarah Stacy.

Children of Deborah Darling and Henry Bosworth are:

149   i.   Elizabeth Bosworth, born 1733.
150   ii.   Mary Bosworth, born 1737.

| 151 | iii. | Rachel Bosworth, born 1739. |
| 152 | iv. | Eunice Bosworth, born 1742. |

34. Anna[4] Darling (Captain John[3], Denice[2], George[1]) was born 20 April 1689 in Mendon, Massachusetts, and died 02 January 1753 in Rehoboth, Massachusetts. She married **Samuel Brown** 08 October 1708 in Mendon, Massachusetts, son of John Brown and Anna Mason. He was born 31 January 1676/77.

Children of Anna Darling and Samuel Brown are:

	153	i.	Samuel Brown, born 04 September 1709 in Rehoboth, Massachusetts; died 1745.
+	154	ii.	Ichabod Brown, born 31 March 1711 in Rehoboth, Massachusetts.
	155	iii.	Martha Brown, born 26 November 1712 in Rehoboth, Massachusetts; died 1752 in Rehoboth, Massachusetts.
	156	iv.	Anna Brown, born 11 February 1713/14. She married John Tillinghast 10 November 1731.
	157	v.	John Brown, born 24 November 1716.
	158	vi.	Peter Brown, born 31 March 1719 in Rehoboth, Massachusetts.
	159	vii.	Abigail Brown, born 05 December 1720.
+	160	viii.	Gideon Brown, born 10 December 1722.
	161	ix.	Lydia Brown, born 16 July 1724.

38. David[4] Darling (Cornelius[3], Denice[2], George[1]) was born 1697 in Attleboro, Massachusetts, and died 02 June 1751 in Bellingham, Massachusetts. He married **Lydia Ware** 1724, daughter of Eleazer Ware and Mary.

Children of David Darling and Lydia Ware are:

	162	i.	Ruhamah Darling, born 07 February 1724/25 in Wrentham, Massachusetts; died 03 March 1740/41 in Wrentham, Massachusetts.
+	163	ii.	Enoch Darling, born 29 September 1727 in Wrentham, Massachusetts; died 10 September 1792 in Bellingham, Massachusetts.
	164	iii.	David Darling, born 26 August 1729 in Wrentham, Massachusetts; died 07 February 1740/41 in Wrentham, Massachusetts.

+ 165   iv.   Timothy Darling, born 14 April 1731 in Wrentham, Massachusetts; died 1784 in Grafton, Massachusetts.

166   v.   Lydia Darling, born 1733 in Wrentham, Massachusetts; died 28 October 1741 in Wrentham, Massachusetts.

167   vi.   Elizabeth Darling, born 1735 in Wrentham, Massachusetts; died 23 February 1740/41 in Wrentham, Massachusetts.

168   vii.   Rachel Darling, born 1737 in Wrentham, Massachusetts; died 20 February 1740/41 in Wrentham, Massachusetts.

169   viii.   Elijah Darling, born 03 February 1739/40 in Wrentham, Massachusetts.

170   ix.   Ruhamah Darling, born 03 December 1742 in Wrentham, Massachusetts.

39. Cornelius[4] Darling (Cornelius[3], Denice[2], George[1]) was born 14 June 1698 in Mendon, Massachusetts, and died 17 February 1783 in Bellingham, Massachusetts. He married **Hannah Thompson** 1723 in Mendon, Massachusetts, daughter of John Thompson and Hannah Wight. She was born 21 April 1692 in Mendon, Massachusetts.

Children of Cornelius Darling and Hannah Thompson are:

171   i.   Mary Darling, born 25 July 1724 in Bellingham, Massachusetts; died 04 January 1760 in Bellingham, Massachusetts. She married Enoch Hill 26 December 1747.

172   ii.   Huldah Darling, born 29 October 1725 in Bellingham, Massachusetts; died 27 March 1763 in Bellingham, Massachusetts.

     Notes for Huldah Darling
     Huldah Darling is buried at the Center Street Cemetery, located on Center Street in Bellingham, Massachusetts

+ 173   iii.   Job Darling, born 02 January 1726/27 in Bellingham, Massachusetts; died 26 March 1814 in Framingham, Massachusetts.

+ 174   iv.   Cornelius Darling, born 15 March 1731/32 in Bellingham, Massachusetts; died 22 March 1816 in Bellingham, Massachusetts.

175   v.   Phebe Darling, born 14 November 1735 in Bellingham, Massachusetts; died 05 May 1761 in Bellingham, Massachusetts.

     Notes for Phebe Darling

Phebe Darling is buried at the Center Street Cemetery, located on Center Street in Bellingham, Massachusetts

40. Richard[4] Darling (Cornelius[3], Denice[2], George[1]) was born 09 December 1700 in Rehoboth, Massachusetts. He married **(1)** ------ **Capron**. He married **(2) Martha Bartlett Staples** 1738.

Child of Richard Darling and ----- Capron is:
  176   i.   Amey Darling, born 1729.

Child of Richard Darling and Martha Staples is:
  177   i.   Ebenezer Darling, born 1740 in Bellingham, Massachusetts.

43. Jane[4] Darling (Cornelius[3], Denice[2], George[1]) was born 17 December 1721 in Bellingham, Massachusetts. She married **Philip Renoff** 18 June 1752 in Rehoboth, Massachusetts.

Children of Jane Darling and Philip Renoff are:
  178   i.   Sarah Renoff.
  179   ii.   Elizabeth Renoff.
  180   iii.   Mary Renoff.

44. John[4] Martin (Hannah[3] Darling, Denice[2], George[1]) was born 14 May 1703.

Child of John Martin is:
  +   181   i.   Susannah[5] Martin.

47. Abigail[4] Darling (Daniel[3], Denice[2], George[1]) was born 11 October 1706 in Mendon, Massachusetts, and died 1747 in Mendon, Massachusetts. She married **John Thayer** 27 July 1727 in Mendon, Massachusetts, son of Isaac Thayer and Mary.

Children of Abigail Darling and John Thayer are:

+	182	i.	Silas[5] Thayer, born 1731.
	183	ii.	Lydia Thayer, born 1735.
	184	iii.	Jesse Thayer.

48. Daniel[4] Darling (Daniel[3], Denice[2], George[1]) was born 28 March 1709 in Mendon, Massachusetts, and died May 1778 in Mendon, Massachusetts. He married **Mary Hunt** 07 September 1732 in Mendon, Massachusetts. She was born 1712 in Smithfield, Rhode Island.

Children of Daniel Darling and Mary Hunt are:

	185	i.	Abner[5] Darling, born 07 March 1731/32 in Mendon, Massachusetts. He married (1) Martha. He married (2) Hannah.
+	186	ii.	Jesse Darling, born 1743 in Mendon, Massachusetts; died 09 July 1813 in Mendon, Massachusetts.
+	187	iii.	Matthew Darling, born 1745 in Mendon, Massachusetts.
+	188	iv.	Mary Darling, born 04 September 1752 in Mendon, Massachusetts; died 24 December 1841.
	189	v.	Lydia Darling, born 1755 in Mendon, Massachusetts. She married Gersham Keith.

49. Lydia[4] Darling (Daniel[3], Denice[2], George[1]) was born 05 January 1710/11 in Mendon, Massachusetts. She married **Benjamin Boyce** 1738, son of Benjamin Boyce and Susanna Bacon. He was born 1710 in Mendon, Massachusetts.

Child of Lydia Darlingand Benjamin Boyce is:

	190	i.	Daniel[5] Boyce, born 1739.

50. Samuel[4] Darling (Daniel[3], Denice[2], George[1]) was born 18 March 1713/14 in Mendon, Massachusetts, and died 1795 in Mendon, Massachusetts. He married **Sarah Benson** 10 January 1745/46 in Smithfield, Rhode Island, daughter of Job Benson and Miriam. She was born 26 September 1730 in Smithfield, Rhode Island.

Children of Samuel Darling and Sarah Benson are:

+	191	i.	Job[5] Darling, born 1749 in Mendon, Massachusetts; died 27 November 1836 in Sutton, Massachusetts.
	192	ii.	Susannah Darling, born 1753 in Mendon, Massachusetts. She married Amos Fairbanks 26 September 1775 in Douglas, Massachusetts.
	193	iii.	Rachel Darling, born 1755 in Mendon, Massachusetts. She married Daniel Sheppard 15 November 1772.
	194	iv.	Leah Darling, born 1757 in Mendon, Massachusetts. She married Benjamin Owen 10 November 1776.
+	195	v.	David Darling, born 21 October 1760 in Mendon, Massachusetts; died 24 August 1829 in New York.
	196	vi.	Abigail Darling, born 1767 in Mendon, Massachusetts. She married John Aldrich 20 February 1790.
	197	vii.	Sarah Darling, born 1770 in Mendon, Massachusetts. She married Joseph Southwick.
+	198	viii.	Benson Darling, born 1772 in Mendon, Massachusetts; died 23 February 1842 in Mendon, Massachusetts.

51. Susannah[4] Darling (Daniel[3], Denice[2], George[1]) was born 02 August 1717 in Mendon, Massachusetts, and died 1778 in Douglas, Massachusetts. She married **(1) David Thompson** 11 October 1737 in Smithfield, Rhode Island, son of David Thompson and Mercy Thayer. He was born 02 December 1711 in Mendon, Massachusetts, and died 1757 in Mendon, Massachusetts. She married **(2) Samuel Humes** 05 March 1759 in Douglas, Massachusetts, son of Nicholas Humes and Margaret. He was born 30 January 1718/19, and died 1806.

Children of Susannah Darling and David Thompson are:

	199	i.	Mary[5] Thompson, born 1740.
	200	ii.	Daniel Thompson, born 30 May 1742.
	201	iii.	Lydia Thompson, born 30 May 1742.
	202	iv.	Susannah Thompson, born 1747.
	203	v.	Sarah Thompson, born 1748.
	204	vi.	David Thompson, born 01 July 1750 in Mendon, Massachusetts; died 10 April 1815 in Mendon, Massachusetts.
	205	vii.	Elisha Thompson, born 1752.
	206	viii.	Susanna Thompson, born 1752.
+	207	ix.	Jemima Thompson, born 1755.
	208	x.	Hezekiah Thompson, born 1757.

52. Kezia⁴ Darling (Daniel³, Denice², George¹) was born 30 November 1719 in Mendon, Massachusetts, and died 1801. She married **John Hunt** 06 June 1738 in Smithfield, Rhode Island. He was born 22 January 1706/07 in Glocester, Rhode Island.

Children of Kezia Darling and John Hunt are:

	209	i.	John⁵ Hunt, born 1739.
	210	ii.	Seth Hunt, born 21 January 1741/42.
+	211	iii.	Keziah Hunt, born 1745.
	212	iv.	George Hunt, born 1747.
	213	v.	Daniel Hunt, born 1751.
+	214	vi.	Peter Hunt, born 1753.
	215	vii.	Rhoda Hunt, born 1755.

54. William⁴ Darling (Daniel³, Denice², George¹) was born 15 January 1729/30 in Mendon, Massachusetts, and died 26 July 1819 in Sutton, Massachusetts. He married **Rachel White** 14 May 1757 in Uxbridge, Massachusetts, daughter of John White and Rachel. She was born 10 March 1738/39 in Mendon, Massachusetts.

Children of William Darling and Rachel White are:

	216	i.	Levi⁵ Darling, born 1758 in Mendon, Massachusetts. He married (1) Dorothy Colby. He married (2) Charlotte Bowman.
	217	ii.	Lavina Darling, born 15 December 1760 in Mendon, Massachusetts; died 27 October 1843. She married Timothy Engley 24 November 1778 in Mendon, Massachusetts.
+	218	iii.	Zeleck Darling, born 05 June 1762 in Mendon, Massachusetts; died 28 January 1844 in Sutton, Massachusetts.
	219	iv.	Trial Darling, born 1766 in Mendon, Massachusetts. She married William Prentice.
+	220	v.	Ehud Darling, born 1768 in Mendon, Massachusetts; died in New York.
	221	vi.	Mary Darling, born 1769 in Mendon, Massachusetts; died 28 September 1819.
+	222	vii.	Aaron Darling, born 1771 in Mendon, Massachusetts; died 24 January 1849.

223	viii.	Christina Darling, born 1773 in Mendon, Massachusetts. She married John Claflin.
224	ix.	Lydia Darling, born 1774 in Mendon, Massachusetts. She married Samuel Crossman.
+ 225	x.	William Darling, born 1776 in Mendon, Massachusetts.
226	xi.	Rachel Darling, born 1780 in Mendon, Massachusetts. She married Levi Prentice.
227	xii.	Abigail Darling, born 1784 in Mendon, Massachusetts. She married John Williams.

58. Obadiah[4] Wheelock (Elizabeth[3] Darling, Denice[2], George[1]) was born 21 September 1712 in Mendon, Massachusetts. He married **Martha Sumner** 26 October 1733 in Mendon, Massachusetts. She was born 27 August 1710 in Mendon, Massachusetts.

Child of Obadiah Wheelock and Martha Sumner is:

| + 228 | i. | Elias[5] Wheelock, born 17 April 1743 in Mendon, Massachusetts; died 1821. |

62. Josiah[4] Wheelock (Elizabeth[3] Darling, Denice[2], George[1]) was born 30 March 1725 in Mendon, Massachusetts, and died 28 December 1794 in Milford, Massachusetts. He married **Experience Clark** 06 January 1746/47 in Mendon, Massachusetts.

Children of Josiah Wheelock and Experience Clark are:

229	i.	Experience[5] Wheelock, born 15 May 1748 in Mendon, Massachusetts
230	ii.	Eleazer Wheelock, born 02 February 1749/50 in Mendon, Massachusetts.
231	iii.	Thankful Wheelock born 07 May 1752 in Mendon, Massachusetts.
232	iv.	Alexander Wheelock, born 02 September 1754 in Mendon, Massachusetts.
+ 233	v.	Bathsheba Wheelock, born 14 December 1760 in Mendon, Massachusetts; died 04 November 1816.
234	vi.	Josiah Wheelock, born 12 August 1763 in Mendon, Massachusetts
235	vii.	Olive Wheelock, born 03 April 1769 in Mendon, Massachusetts.

236   viii.   Obadiah Wheelock, born 06 April 1771 in Mendon, Massachusetts.

63. Samuel[4] Wheelock (Elizabeth[3] Darling, Denice[2], George[1]) was born 06 September 1714 in Mendon, Massachusetts. He married **Hannah Amidon** 16 February 1736/37 in Mendon, Massachusetts, daughter of Philip Amidon and Ithamar Warfield. She was born 02 February 1716/17 in Mendon, Massachusetts, and died 27 December 1803 in Mendon, Massachusetts.

Children of Samuel Wheelock and Hannah Amidon are:

237   i.   Mary[5] Wheelock, born 31 December 1738 in Mendon, Massachusetts She married Caleb Cheney 09 May 1758 in Mendon, Massachusetts

238   ii.   Samuel Wheelock born 11 September 1743 in Mendon, Massachusetts; died in YOUNG.

239   iii.   Samuel Wheelock born 22 September 1745.

240   iv.   Elizabeth Wheelock, born 31 August 1748.

241   v.   Hannah Wheelock, born 31 August 1748.

242   vi.   Rachel Wheelock, born 11 February 1749/50.

243   vii.   Levi Wheelock, born 03 August 1755 in Milford, Massachusetts. He married Waitstill.

244   viii.   Isabel Wheelock, born 09 May 1757.

245   ix.   Amariah Wheelock, born 15 May 1759

246   x.   Obadiah Wheelock, born 20 April 1762.

67. Deborah[4] Darling (Benjamin[3], Denice[2], George[1]) was born 22 April 1711 in Mendon, Massachusetts. She married **Daniel Wheelock** 30 March 1732 in Uxbridge, Massachusetts, son of Benjamin Wheelock and Huldah Thayer. He was born 20 December 1707 in Mendon, Massachusetts

Children of Deborah Darling and Daniel Wheelock are:

247   i.   Mary[5] Wheelock, born 14 January 1733/34 in Uxbridge, Massachusetts.

+ 248   ii.   Paul Wheelock, born 09 February 1736/37 in Uxbridge, Massachusetts.

| 249 | iii. | Hannah Wheelock, born 13 December 1741. She married Henry Keith 27 September 1760 in Uxbridge, Massachusetts. |
+ | 250 | iv. | Daniel Wheelock, born 13 August 1744. |
251	v.	Mary Wheelock born 20 September 1746. She married Joseph Albee; born 1761 in Dudley, Massachusetts.
252	vi.	Rhoda Wheelock, born 1750.
253	vii.	Deborah Wheelock, born 1753.

68. Benjamin[4] Darling (Benjamin[3], Denice[2], George[1]) was born 15 March 1713/14 in Mendon, Massachusetts. He married **Elizabeth Force** 28 July 1733 in Smithfield, Rhode Island. She was born 1714 in Mendon, Massachusetts.

Children of Benjamin Darling and Elizabeth Force are:

254	i.	Aaron[5] Darling, born 1734 in New York.
255	ii.	James Darling, born 1736.
256	iii.	John Darling, born 29 April 1739.
257	iv.	Moses Darling, born 1741.
258	v.	Ephraim Darling, born 1743.
259	vi.	Benjamin Darling, born 1744.
260	vii.	Jonathan Darling, born 1745.

69. Joseph[4] Darling (Benjamin[3], Denice[2], George[1]) was born 21 April 1716 in Mendon, Massachusetts, and died 1787 in Mendon, Massachusetts. He married **Mary Fish** 06 January 1732/33 in Smithfield, Rhode Island, daughter of John Fish and Mary Lewis. She was born 25 May 1712 in Reading, Massachusetts.

Children of Joseph Darling and Mary Fish are:

+ | 261 | i. | Joseph[5] Darling, born 06 April 1736 in Mendon, Massachusetts. |
+ | 262 | ii. | Stephen Darling, born 21 August 1738 in Mendon, Massachusetts; died in Richmond, New Hampshire. |
+ | 263 | iii. | Lydia Darling, born 21 April 1743 in Mendon, Massachusetts; died 12 July 1807 in New Hampshire. |
+ | 264 | iv. | Enoch Darling, born 08 July 1746 in Mendon, Massachusetts. |

265	v.	Elijah Darling, born 19 May 1748 in Mendon, Massachusetts. He married Sarah Washburn 13 April 1769 in Mendon, Massachusetts.
266	vi.	Mary Darling, born 11 February 1748/49; died 14 June 1814. She married Noble Baggs 30 April 1768 in Uxbridge, Massachusetts; born 20 April 1745.
+ 267	vii.	Jacob Darling, born 02 December 1751 in Mendon, Massachusetts; died 01 February 1822 in Indiana.

70. Ebenezer[4] Darling (Benjamin[3], Denice[2], George[1]) was born 25 August 1718 in Mendon, Massachusetts, and died 25 November 1806 in Glocester, Rhode Island. He married **Mary Hakes** 25 February 1743/44 in Smithfield, Rhode Island, daughter of Solomon Hakes and Anna Billings. She was born 1725.

Notes for Ebenezer Darling:
Ebenezer Darling is buried at the Darling Lot, located on Sprague Hill Road in Glocester, Rhode Island

Children of Ebenezer Darling and Mary Hakes are:
+	268	i.	David[5] Darling, born 1747 in Glocester, Rhode Island; died 1823 in North Adams, Massachusetts.
+	269	ii.	Andrew Darling, born 22 May 1749 in Glocester, Rhode Island; died 02 August 1790 in Burrillville, Rhode Island.
	270	iii.	John Darling, born 1750.
+	271	iv.	Ebenezer Darling, born June 1751 in Glocester, Rhode Island; died December 1820 in Glocester, Rhode Island.
+	272	v.	Dorcas Darling, born 09 July 1759 in Glocester, Rhode Island; died 16 September 1852 in Glocester, Rhode Island.
	273	vi.	Mary Darling, born 1761 in Glocester, Rhode Island.
	274	vii.	Elizabeth Darling, born 1763 in Glocester, Rhode Island.
+	275	viii.	Martha Darling, born 1765 in Glocester, Rhode Island; died 1847 in Glocester, Rhode Island.
	276	ix.	Deborah Darling, born 1767 in Glocester, Rhode Island.
	277	x.	Rachel Darling, born 1769 in Glocester, Rhode Island.

71. Peter[4] Darling (Benjamin[3], Denice[2], George[1]) was born 12 June 1720 in Mendon, Massachusetts, and died 16 May 1818 in Cumberland, Rhode Island. He married **(1) Priscilla Cook** 20

April 1749 in Mendon, Massachusetts, daughter of Daniel Cook and Susannah. She was born 1720 in Mendon, Massachusetts. He married (2) **Anne Cook** 12 June 1768 in Cumberland, Rhode Island, daughter of Elder Cook and Mary Staples. She was born 03 December 1749 in Mendon, Massachusetts. He married (3) **Amey Wilkinson** 20 August 1772, daughter of John Wilkinson and Rebecca Scott. She was born 23 January 1718/19.

Children of Peter Darling and Priscilla Cook are:

278	i.	Stephen[5] Darling, born 06 May 1750 in Cumberland, Rhode Island; died 11 October 1756 in Cumberland, Rhode Island.
279	ii.	Richard Darling, born 16 September 1753 in Cumberland, Rhode Island; died 17 October 1756 in Cumberland, Rhode Island.
+ 280	iii.	Peter Darling, born 22 August 1757 in Cumberland, Rhode Island; died 13 November 1796 in Cumberland, Rhode Island.

Children of Peter Darling and Anne Cook are:

+ 281	i.	Darius[5] Darling, born 21 May 1769 in Cumberland, Rhode Island.
282	ii.	Luke Darling, born 21 July 1770 in Cumberland, Rhode Island.
283	iii.	Anna Darling, born 02 August 1771 in Cumberland, Rhode Island; died 01 March 1772.

Children of Peter Darling and Amey Wilkinson are:

284	i.	Ruth[5] Darling, born 1731 in Bellingham, Massachusetts. She married Timothy Darling 09 July 1758 in Cumberland, Rhode Island; born 30 January 1725/26 in Bellingham, Massachusetts.
+ 285	ii.	Welcome Darling, born in Cumberland, Rhode Island.
286	iii.	Elijah Darling, born 10 July 1773 in Cumberland, Rhode Island. He married Lucy Cook 07 January 1798 in Cumberland, Rhode Island.
+ 287	iv.	Benjamin Darling, born 23 July 1774 in Cumberland, Rhode Island.
288	v.	Joannah Darling, born 03 January 1776 in Cumberland, Rhode Island. She married Jonathan Wilkinson 19 November 1797 in Cumberland, Rhode Island.

+ 289   vi.   Reuben Darling, born December 1779 in Cumberland,
                   Rhode Island; died 04 July 1869.
   290   vii. Welcome Darling. He married Sarah Goodale.

72. Hannah[4] Darling (Benjamin[3], Denice[2], George[1]) was
born 25 March 1722 in Mendon, Massachusetts, and died 07
February 1799 in Mendon, Massachusetts. She married **Jeremiah
Battles** 1742 in Mendon, Massachusetts, son of Edward Battles
and Experience Pratt. He was born 16 May 1719 in Mendon,
Massachusetts.

Children of Hannah Darling and Jeremiah Battles are:
   291   i.   Edward[5] Battles, born 13 January 1742/43 in Mendon,
                   Massachusetts.
   292   ii.   Hannah Battles, born 1744.
   293   iii. Susanna Battles, born 04 July 1746.
   294   iv.   Jeremiah Battles, born 1748.

73. Abigail[4] Darling (Benjamin[3], Denice[2], George[1]) was born
15 March 1723/24 in Mendon, Massachusetts, and died 03 August
1809 in Burrillville, Rhode Island. She married **Elisha Inman** 16
January 1743/44 in Glocester, Rhode Island, son of Edward Inman
and Mary Malowery. He was born September 1719 in Glocester,
Rhode Island.

Children of Abigail Darling and Elisha Inman are:
   295   i.   Susannah[5] Inman, born 1749 in Glocester, Rhode Island.
   296   ii   Abigail Inman born 1751 in Glocester, Rhode Island.
   297   iii. Penelope Inman' born 1753 in Glocester, Rhode Island.
   298   iv.   Anna Inman, born 1755 in Glocester, Rhode Island.
   299   v.   Samuel Inman, born 1755 in Glocester, Rhode Island.
   300   vi.   Elisha Inman, born 1757.
   301   vii. Martha Inman, born 1757.
   302   viii. Priscilla Inman, born 1758.
   303   ix.   Mary Inman' born 1761.
   304   x.   Elizabeth Inman, born 1763 in Glocester, Rhode Island.

74. Samuel[4] Darling (Benjamin[3], Denice[2], George[1]) was born 01 August 1726 in Mendon, Massachusetts, and died 1763 in Millville, Massachusetts. He married **(1) Esther Slack**. He married **(2) Sarah White** 01 April 1746 in Mendon, Massachusetts, daughter of John White and Sarah Cheney. She was born 08 November 1724 in Mendon, Massachusetts.

Child of Samuel Darling and Esther Slack is:
+   305   i.   Lucy[5] Darling, born 15 August 1772 in Bellingham, Massachusetts; died 1830.

Children of Samuel Darling and Sarah White are:
    306   i.   Mehitable[5] Darling, born 07 September 1746 in Mendon, Massachusetts. She married (1) Ebenezer Knapp. She married (2) Joseph Howe 1770.

    307   ii.   Deborah Darling, born 06 July 1750 in Mendon, Massachusetts. She married John Hunt; born 09 October 1741 in Mendon, Massachusetts, born in Uxbridge, Massachusetts.

+   308   iii.   Peter Darling, born 20 January 1752 in Mendon, Massachusetts; died June 1822 in Rowe, Massachusetts.

    309   iv.   Trial Darling, born 20 May 1754 in Mendon, Massachusetts. She married Wilson Pintas 21 June 1784 in Mendon, Massachusetts.

    310   v.   Aaron Darling, born 20 June 1756 in Mendon, Massachusetts. He married Huldah Blake 17 November 1783 in Mendon, Massachusetts.

    311   vi.   Dinnis Darling, born 20 February 1760 in Mendon, Massachusetts. He married Deborah Balcom 16 December 1782 in Mendon, Massachusetts.

+   312   vii.   Henry Darling, born 03 July 1762 in Mendon, Massachusetts.

+   313   viii.   Caleb Darling, born 30 November 1748 in Mendon, Massachusetts.

75. Elizabeth[4] Darling (Benjamin[3], Denice[2], George[1]) was born 11 April 1729 in Mendon, Massachusetts, and died 23 March 1778 in Mendon, Massachusetts. She married **Benjamin Medbury** 08 December 1748 in Mendon, Massachusetts, son of

Nathaniel Medbury and Dorothy. He was born 31 March 1727 in Warwick, Rhode Island.

Children of Elizabeth Darling and Benjamin Medbury are:
314   i.   Edward[5] Medbury, born 1749.
315   ii. Nathan Medbury, born 1751.
316   iii. Benjamin Medbury, born 1753.
317   iv. Darling Medbury , born 1755.
318   v.   Nathaniel Medbury, born 1757.
319   vi. Joseph Medbury, born 1759.
320   vii. David Medbury, born 1761.
321   viii. Isaac Medbury, born 1763.
322   ix. Ruth Medbury, born 1765.
323   x.   Mary Medbury, born 1768.

76. Thomas[4] Darling (Benjamin[3], Denice[2], George[1]) was born 07 May 1730 in Mendon, Massachusetts, and died 22 October 1776 in Mendon, Massachusetts. He married **Rachel White** 04 December 1749 in Mendon, Massachusetts, daughter of Joseph White and Prudence Smith. She was born 14 November 1732 in Uxbridge, Massachusetts.

Notes for Thomas Darling:
Thomas Darling is buried at the Chestnut Hill Meeting House Cemetery, located on Chestnut Hill Road in Millville, Massachusetts

Children of Thomas Darling and Rachel White are:
324   i.   Rhoda[5] Darling, born 08 May 1750 in Mendon, Massachusetts; died 25 June 1842 in New York. She married Jepthah Clark 01 December 1768 in Mendon, Massachusetts; born 28 February 1742/43.
+ 325   ii. Joanna Darling, born 01 February 1752 in Mendon, Massachusetts.
+ 326   iii. Rachel Darling, born 01 May 1754 in Mendon, Massachusetts.
327   iv. Prudence Darling, born 28 September 1757 in Mendon, Massachusetts; died 10 July 1827. She married Nabor Staples 04 February 1775 in Mendon, Massachusetts; born 1756.

+	328	v.	Seth Darling, born 21 March 1760 in Mendon, Massachusetts; died 27 March 1825 in Vermont.
+	329	vi.	Simeon Darling, born 21 March 1764 in Mendon, Massachusetts.
	330	vii.	Benjamin Darling, born 28 February 1766 in Mendon, Massachusetts.
+	331	viii.	John Darling, born 09 June 1768 in Mendon, Massachusetts.
+	332	ix.	Nathan Darling, born 17 December 1770 in Mendon, Massachusetts; died 07 September 1855 in Hopedale, Massachusetts.
+	333	x.	Alpheus Darling, born 07 November 1773 in Mendon, Massachusetts.

77. Deborah[4] Darling (Benjamin[3], Denice[2], George[1]) was born 22 April 1711 in Mendon, Massachusetts. She married **Daniel Wheelock** 30 March 1732 in Mendon, Massachusetts, son of Benjamin Wheelock and Huldah Thayer. He was born 20 December 1707 in Mendon, Massachusetts.

Children of Deborah Darling and Daniel Wheelock are:

	334	i.	Mary[5] Wheelock, born 14 January 1732/33 in Uxbridge, Massachusetts
	335	ii.	Paul Wheelock born 09 February 1738/39 in Uxbridge, Massachusetts. He married (1) Lydia Sayles 1763. He married (2) Deborah Morse 30 August 1784 in Uxbridge, Massachusetts.
	336	iii.	Rhoda Wheelock, born 28 December 1758 in Uxbridge, Massachusetts[25]. She married Enoch Aldrich.

78. Anna[4] Darling (Benjamin[3], Denice[2], George[1]) was born 22 June 1761 in Mendon, Massachusetts. She married **Benjamin Carrell** 06 September 1779 in Mendon, Massachusetts.

Children of Anna Darling and Benjamin Carrell are:

	337	i.	Benjamin[5] Carrell.
	338	ii.	James Carrell.
	339	iii.	Jared Carrell.
	340	iv.	Joseph Carrell.

80. Mary⁵ Darling (John⁴, Captain John³, Denice², George¹) was born 02 March 1711/12. She married **Ichabod Brown** 09 September 1736 in Rehoboth, Massachusetts, son of Samuel Brown and Anna Darling. He was born 31 March 1711 in Rehoboth, Massachusetts.

Child of Mary Darlingand Ichabod Brown is:

    341   i.   Lydia⁶ Brown, born 21 March 1735/36 in Rehoboth, Massachusetts.

81. Elizabeth⁵ Darling (John⁴, Captain John³, Denice², George¹) was born 07 November 1712 in Mendon, Massachusetts. She married **Samuel Hunt** 15 October 1732 in Glocester, Rhode Island.

Children of Elizabeth Darlingand Samuel Hunt are:

    342   i.   John⁶ Hunt, born 17 September 1733 in Mendon, Massachusetts.
    343   ii.   Mary Hunt, born 09 March 1735/36 in Mendon, Massachusetts.
    344   iii. Samuel Hunt, born 02 January 1738/39.
    345   iv. John Hunt, born 09 October 1741 in Mendon, Massachusetts. He married Deborah Darling; born 06 July 1750 in Mendon, Massachusetts.
+   346   v.   Elizabeth Hunt, born 09 June 1744 in Mendon, Massachusetts; died 1790.

82. John⁵ Darling (John⁴, Captain John³, Denice², George¹) was born 01 December 1717 in Mendon, Massachusetts, and died 24 August 1798 in Cumberland, Rhode Island. He married **Hannah Healy** 01 May 1740 in Rehoboth, Massachusetts, daughter of Paul Healy and Hannah Titus. She was born 03 March 1721/22 in Rehoboth, Massachusetts, and died 09 June 1799 in Cumberland, Rhode Island.

Children of John Darling and Hannah Healy are:

+ 347   i.   John[6] Darling, born 24 April 1741 in Wrentham, Massachusetts; died 1820 in Cumberland, Rhode Island.

348   ii.   Esther Darling, born 09 July 1743 in Wrentham, Massachusetts. She married John Knight.

+ 349   iii.   Hannah Darling, born 17 November 1744 in Wrentham, Massachusetts; died 28 November 1819.

350   iv.   James Darling, born 04 August 1746 in Wrentham, Massachusetts; died 08 November 1777 in Wrentham, Massachusetts.

351   v.   Martha Darling, born 16 April 1749 in Wrentham, Massachusetts. She married Joseph Tower.

352   vi.   Mary Darling, born 16 April 1749 in Wrentham, Massachusetts.

353   vii.   Peter Darling, born 16 May 1751 in Wrentham, Massachusetts. He married Persis Robinson.

+ 354   viii.   Rev. David Darling, born 14 April 1753 in Wrentham, Massachusetts; died 15 March 1835 in New Hampshire.

355   ix.   Eunice Darling, born 05 August 1755 in Wrentham, Massachusetts. She married Benjamin Wilmarth.

356   x.   Jemima Darling, born 03 June 1757 in Wrentham, Massachusetts. She married Elias Jones.

357   xi.   Jerusha Darling, born 03 June 1757 in Wrentham, Massachusetts. She married Ephraim Whiting.

+ 358   xii.   Elias Darling, born 03 December 1759 in Wrentham, Massachusetts.

359   xiii.   Susanna Darling, born 1761 in Wrentham, Massachusetts. She married Simon Fisher.

+ 360   xiv.   Abel Darling, born 05 October 1766 in Wrentham, Massachusetts; died 30 December 1826 in Medway, Massachusetts.

83. Pelatiah[5] Darling (John[4], Captain John[3], Denice[2], George[1]) was born 28 February 1719/20 in Mendon, Massachusetts, and died 30 June 1796 in Mendon, Massachusetts. He married **Elizabeth Darling** 29 December 1743 in Medway, Massachusetts, daughter of Samuel Darling and Mary Thompson. She was born 31 August 1725 in Bellingham, Massachusetts, and died 09 May 1809 in Medway, Massachusetts.

Children of Pelatiah Darling and Elizabeth Darling are:

361	i.	Mary[6] Darling, born 14 May 1745 in Mendon, Massachusetts; died May 1809 in Blackstone, Massachusetts.
362	ii.	John Darling, born 27 July 1747 in Mendon, Massachusetts. He married Elizabeth Warfield; born 1751.
363	iii.	Hannah Darling, born 07 December 1750 in Mendon, Massachusetts. She married John Benson.
364	iv.	Elizabeth Darling, born 08 February 1753 in Mendon, Massachusetts; died March 1811 in Blackstone, Massachusetts.
365	v.	Abigail Darling, born 15 April 1755 in Mendon, Massachusetts; died 01 November 1824 in Blackstone, Massachusetts.
366	vi.	Rachel Darling, born 14 March 1758 in Mendon, Massachusetts. She married Samuel Benson 1780 in Mendon, Massachusetts; born 1757.
+ 367	vii.	Pelatiah Darling, born 02 April 1760 in Mendon, Massachusetts; died 03 April 1839 in Mendon, Massachusetts.
+ 368	viii.	Joshua Darling, born 19 August 1762 in Mendon, Massachusetts; died 21 April 1834 in Uxbridge, Massachusetts.
369	ix.	Seth Darling, born 1764 in Mendon, Massachusetts.
370	x.	Ruth Darling, born 05 June 1766 in Mendon, Massachusetts; died 03 October 1846 in Millville, Massachusetts.
+ 371	xi.	Phineas Darling, born 20 March 1769 in Mendon, Massachusetts; died 1818 in Burrillville, Rhode Island.

85. Ruth[5] Darling (John[4], Captain John[3], Denice[2], George[1]) was born 01 July 1726 in Mendon, Massachusetts. She married **Joseph Albee** 08 November 1744 in Smithfield, Rhode Island, son of Benjamin Albee and Abial Wheelock. He was born 1718 in Uxbridge, Massachusetts.

Children of Ruth Darling and Joseph Albee are:

372	i.	Benjamin[6] Albee, born 1740 in Burrillville, Rhode Island; died 02 July 1818 in Charlton, Massachusetts. He married Sarah Taft 1768; born 08 March 1749/50 in Uxbridge, Massachusetts.
373	ii.	Ruth Albee.
374	iii.	Abial Albee. She married John White.
375	iv.	John Albee.

+	376	v.	Joseph Albee, born 1751; died 07 May 1819 in Oxford, Massachusetts.
	377	vi.	Aaron Albee, born 03 April 1762; died 29 October 1802 in Dudley, Massachusetts. He married Martha Willard; born 17 May 1766 in Dudley, Massachusetts.

86. Abigail⁵ Thayer (Abigail⁴ Darling, Captain John³, Denice², George¹) was born 1730 in Mendon, Massachusetts and died 1790. She married **Noah Thayer**, son of Captain Thayer and Sarah Wheelock. He was born 04 May 1730 in Mendon, Massachusetts, and died 28 July 1790.

Child of Abigail Thayer and Noah Thayer is:

	378	i.	Elijah⁶ Thayer born 24 April 1753 in Mendon, Massachusetts; died 22 October 1820. He married Hannah Huntley; born 1756.

88. Elizabeth⁵ Thayer (Ruth⁴ Darling, Captain John³, Denice², George¹) was born 17 February 1723/24 in Uxbridge, Massachusetts, and died 27 August 1797 in Uxbridge, Massachusetts. She married **Joseph Taft** 23 June 1741 in Uxbridge, Massachusetts, son of Joseph Taft and Elizabeth Emerson. He was born 19 April 1722 in Uxbridge, Massachusetts.

Child of Elizabeth Thayer and Joseph Taft is:

+	379	i.	Reuben⁶ Taft, born 21 October 1742 in Uxbridge, Massachusetts.

89. Deacon Samuel⁵ Darling (Captain Samuel⁴, Captain John³, Denice², George¹) was born 19 January 1718/19, and died 12 June 1814. He married **Esther Slack** 20 January 1755. She was born. 1736, and died 18 February 1816.

Children of Deacon Darling and Esther Slack are:
- 380   i.   Lucy[6] Darling, born 15 August 1772.
- 381   ii. Sabra Darling, born 15 April 1774.
- 382   iii. Oliver Darling, born 30 March 1779[27]; died 05 June 1848.

96. Joseph[5] Darling (Ebenezer[4], Captain John[3], Denice[2], George[1]) was born 29 July 1722 in Bellingham, Massachusetts. He married **Bathsheba Inman** 26 August 1750 in Cumberland, Rhode Island, daughter of Joseph Inman and Deborah Smith. She was born 1726 in Providence, Rhode Island.

Children of Joseph Darling and Bathsheba Inman are:
- + 383   i.   Bathsheba[6] Darling, born 30 January 1752 in Cumberland, Rhode Island.
- 384   ii. Phebe Darling, born 10 December 1753 in Cumberland, Rhode Island. She married Stephen Estes 19 May 1774 in Cumberland, Rhode Island.
- 385   iii. Ebenezer Darling, born 30 October 1756 in Cumberland, Rhode Island.
- 386   iv. Abigail Darling, born 02 June 1760 in Cumberland, Rhode Island.
- 387   v. Lucy Darling, born 03 July 1764 in Cumberland, Rhode Island.

98. Timothy[5] Darling (Ebenezer[4], Captain John[3], Denice[2], George[1]) was born 30 January 1725/26 in Bellingham, Massachusetts. He married **(1) Kezia**. She was born in Bellingham, Massachusetts. He married **(2) Ruth Darling** 09 July 1758 in Cumberland, Rhode Island, daughter of Peter Darling and Amey Wilkinson. She was born 1731 in Bellingham, Massachusetts.

Children of Timothy Darlingand Kezia are:
- 388   i.   Mercy[6] Darling, born 22 August 1762 in Bellingham, Massachusetts.
- 389   ii. Joab Darling, born 23 October 1763 in Bellingham, Massachusetts. He married Mary 1791.
- 390   iii. Jemima Darling, born 24 August 1765 in Bellingham, Massachusetts.

| 391 | iv. | Timothy Darling, born 19 April 1767 in Bellingham, Massachusetts. He married Rachel Trask 03 February 1794 in Bellingham, Massachusetts. |
| + 392 | v. | Simeon Darling, born 06 December 1769 in Bellingham, Massachusetts. |

122. Priscilla[5] Thayer (Ruth[4] Darling, Captain John[3], Denice[2], George[1]) was born 06 June 1717 in Mendon, Massachusetts She married **Moses Taft** 03 October 1737 in Uxbridge, Massachusetts, son of Joseph Taft. He was born 30 January 1716/17 in Mendon, Massachusetts, and died 16 July 1778.

Notes for Moses Taft:
Moses Taft is buried at the Prospect Hill Cemetery, located on Route 16 in Uxbridge, Massachusetts

Children of Priscilla Thayer and Moses Taft are:

+ 393	i.	Abner[6] Taft, born 28 December 1736 in Uxbridge, Massachusetts; died 30 May 1809.
394	ii.	Ruth Taft, born 19 February 1739/40 in Uxbridge, Massachusetts. She married Joseph Chapin 09 March 1758 in Uxbridge, Massachusetts; born 29 January 1729/30.
395	iii.	Moses Taft, born 31 December 1742 in Uxbridge, Massachusetts.
396	iv.	Margaret Taft, born 19 February 1743/44 in Uxbridge, Massachusetts. She married Levi White 05 December 1765; born 30 January 1743/44
+ 397	v.	Nahum Taft, born 17 August 1745 in Uxbridge, Massachusetts.
398	vi.	Mary Taft, born 17 July 1747 in Uxbridge, Massachusetts.
399	vii.	Priscilla Taft born 30 July 1749 in Uxbridge, Massachusetts. She married Timothy Taft 06 December 1780.
400	viii.	Luke Taft born 10 August 1754 in Uxbridge, Massachusetts
401	ix.	Joanna Taft, born 26 June 1756 in Uxbridge, Massachusetts; died 30 September 1761 in Uxbridge, Massachusetts.
402	x.	Mary Taft, born 19 July 1761 in Uxbridge, Massachusetts; died 03 October 1761 in Uxbridge, Massachusetts.
403	xi.	James Taft born 09 April 1738.
404	xii.	Margaret Taft, born 19 February 1742/43.
405	xiii.	Moses Taft, born 21 December 1745.
406	xiv.	Joel Taft born 28 May 1747.

407	xv.	Joseph Taft born 06 July 1751
408	xvi.	Josiah Taft, born 17 October 1758
409	xvii.	Margaret Taft, born 19 February 1741/42 in Uxbridge, Massachusetts She married Levi White 05 December 1765; born 30 January 1743/44.
410	xviii.	Moses Taft, born 31 December 1743 in Uxbridge, Massachusetts.
411	xix.	Nathum Taft, born 17 August 1745 in Uxbridge, Massachusetts. He married Rachel Albee 19 February 1767.
412	xx.	Priscilla Taft, born 30 April 1749 in Uxbridge, Massachusetts. She married Timothy Taft 06 December 1780

123. Peter[5] Thayer (Ruth[4] Darling, Captain John[3], Denice[2], George[1]) was born 16 April 1720 in Mendon, Massachusetts. He married **Sarah Holbrook** 12 June 1740 in Mendon, Massachusetts, daughter of Silvanus Holbrook and Naomi Cook. She was born in Uxbridge, Massachusetts.

Children of Peter Thayer and Sarah Holbrook are:

413	i.	Naomi[6] Thayer, born 04 July 1751 in Mendon, Massachusetts. She married Stephen Carrary in Mendon, Massachusetts.
+ 414	ii.	Reuben Thayer, born 27 June 1753; died 09 June 1804 in New York.
415	iii.	Peter Thayer, born 20 October 1755. in Mendon Massachusetts.
416	iv.	Oliver Thayer, born 09 July 1758.
417	v.	Silvanus Thayer, born 04 September 1762. in Mendon, Massachusetts. He married Diana Taft, 4 Feburary 1793.
418	vi.	Hannah Thayer, born 28 July 1764. She married Caleb Taft 09 July 1781 in Mendon, Massachusetts.

132. Samuel[5] Darling (Samuel[4], Captain John[3], Denice[2], George[1]) was born 09 January 1718/19 in Bellingham, Massachusetts, and died 12 June 1814 in Bellingham, Massachusetts. He married **Esther Slack** 10 December 1754 in Bellingham, Massachusetts, daughter of Benjamin Slack and Jerusha Whiting. She was born 1736 in Attleboro, Massachusetts, and died 18 February 1816 in Bellingham, Massachusetts.

Notes for Esther Slack:
Esther Slack is buried at the Center Street Cemetery, located on Center Street in Bellingham, Massachusetts

Children of Samuel Darling and Esther Slack are:

421	i.	Jerusha[6] Darling, born 27 July 1756 in Bellingham, Massachusetts. She married Silas Cook; born 23 March 1753 in Cumberland, Rhode Island; died 12 February 1842.
+ 422	ii.	Joanna Darling, born 10 October 1757 in Bellingham, Massachusetts; died 06 February 1815.
+ 423	iii.	Samuel Darling, born 08 August 1759 in Bellingham, Massachusetts; died 16 January 1851.
424	iv.	Benjamin Darling born 04 July 1761 in Bellingham, Massachusetts; died March 1814. He married (1) Nancy Cook; born 08 July 1768 in Cumberland, Rhode Island He married (2) Celina Cook.
425	v.	Reuben Darling born 12 April 1763 in Bellingham, Massachusetts; died 06 January 1780 in Bellingham, Massachusetts.
426	vi.	Esther Darling, born 01 September 1765 in Bellingham, Massachusetts; died 1864 in Bellingham, Massachusetts. She married (1) Joseph Capron. She married (2) Nathan Arnold 30 November 1786 in Bellingham, Massachusetts; born 1761 in Cumberland, Rhode Island.
+ 427	vii.	Ziba Darling, born 19 September 1767 in Bellingham, Massachusetts; died 29 October 1825 in Providence, Rhode Island.
428	viii.	Nathan Darling, born 10 May 1770 in Bellingham, Massachusetts; died 02 September 1777 in Bellingham, Massachusetts.
429	ix.	Lucy Darling, born 15 August 1772 in Bellingham, Massachusetts. She married Whipple Cook born 23 May 1773 in Cumberland, Rhode Island; died 04 December 1858
430	x.	Sabra Darling, born 25 March 1774 in Bellingham, Massachusetts. She married Ebenezer Thayer.
+ 431	xi.	Rhoda Darling, born 24 September 1776 in Bellingham, Massachusetts; died 08 August 1843 in Bellingham, Massachusetts.
+ 432	xii.	Olive Darling, born 30 June 1779 in Bellingham, Massachusetts; died 1848.
433	xiii.	Milla Darlin[g], born 01 March 1785 in Bellingham, Massachusetts; died 18 May 1786 in Bellingham, Massachusetts.

133. Michael[5] Darling (Samuel[4], Captain John[3], Denice[2], George[1]) was born 06 March 1722/23 in Bellingham, Massachusetts, and died 25 February 1803 in Ballston, New York. He married **Hannah Dixon** 01 May 1755.

Children of Michael Darling and Hannah Dixon are:

434	i.	Mary[6] Darling, born 24 October 1766 in Connecticut.
435	ii.	James Darling, born 27 August 1768 in Connecticut.
436	iii.	John Darling, born 20 April 1771 in Connecticut.
437	iv.	Elizabeth Darling, born 11 July 1774 in Connecticut.
438	v.	Sarah Darling, born 30 October 1777 in Connecticut.

134. Elizabeth[5] Darling (Samuel[4], Captain John[3], Denice[2], George[1]) was born 31 August 1725 in Bellingham, Massachusetts, and died 09 May 1809 in Medway, Massachusetts. She married **Pelatiah Darling** 29 December 1743 in Medway, Massachusetts, son of John Darling and Hannah Staples. He was born 28 February 1719/20 in Mendon, Massachusetts, and died 30 June 1796 in Mendon, Massachusetts.

Children are listed above under (83) Pelatiah Darling

135. Ruth[5] Darling (Samuel[4], Captain John[3], Denice[2], George[1]) was born 03 July 1728 in Bellingham, Massachusetts. She married **John Pitts** 22 September 1747 in Smithfield, Rhode Island.

Children of Ruth Darling and John Pitts are:

439	i.	Elizabeth[6] Pitts, born 1748.
440	ii.	Ignatius Pitts, born 27 May 1750.
441	iii.	Rufus Pitts, born 1752.
442	iv.	Michael Pitts, born 1755.
443	v.	John Pitts, born 1759.
444	vi.	Ruth Pitts, born 1762.

136. Abigail⁵ Darling (Samuel⁴, Captain John³, Denice², George¹) was born 16 February 1730/31 in Bellingham, Massachusetts, and died 23 June 1826 in Bellingham, Massachusetts. She married **Jonathan Draper** 11 April 1753 in Bellingham, Massachusetts, son of Jonathan Draper and Mary Darling. He was born 10 May 1730 in Bellingham, Massachusetts.

Children of Abigail Darlingand Jonathan Draper are:

+   445   i.   Sarah⁶ Draper, born 1754.
     446   ii.   Abigail Draper, born 23 December 1756 in Bellingham, Massachusetts. She married John Chilson 03 January 1782 in Bellingham, Massachusetts.
     447   iii.   Ichabod Draper, born 16 January 1760.
     448   iv.   Jonathan Draper, born 1762.
     449   v.   Rahcel Draper, born 08 March 1762.
+   450   vi.   Molly Draper, born 1766.
     451   vii.   Jotham Draper, born 06 October 1769.

137. John⁵ Darling (Samuel⁴, Captain John³, Denice², George¹) was born 29 April 1733 in Bellingham, Massachusetts, and died 02 February 1800 in Bellingham, Massachusetts. He married **Anna Jillson** 07 November 1755 in Bellingham, Massachusetts, daughter of Uriah Jillson and Sarah Ballou. She was born 14 October 1736 in Cumberland, Rhode Island.

Children of John Darling and Anna Jillson are:

     452   i.   Prudence⁶ Darling, born 26 May 1756 in Bellingham, Massachusetts; died 11 September 1756 in Bellingham, Massachusetts.
     453   ii.   Mary Darling, born 21 July 1757 in Bellingham, Massachusetts. She married John Haskell 01 October 1780 in Cumberland, Rhode Island; born 1750.
     454   iii.   Penelope Darling, born 20 November 1759 in Bellingham, Massachusetts. She married Levi Aldrich 1786 in Bellingham, Massachusetts.
     455   iv.   John Darling, born 01 November 1761 in Bellingham, Massachusetts. He married Levice Cook 19 May 1781 in Bellingham, Massachusetts.

456	v.	Nathaniel Darling, born 11 January 1764 in Bellingham, Massachusetts. He married Seviah Cook 09 January 1792 in Bellingham, Massachusetts.
457	vi.	Sarah Darling, born 12 June 1766 in Bellingham, Massachusetts. She married Reuben Aldrich 02 August 1788 in Bellingham, Massachusetts.
458	vii.	Stephen Darling, born 10 July 1768 in Bellingham, Massachusetts; died 28 June 1773 in Bellingham, Massachusetts.
459	viii.	Anna Darling, born 30 October 1770 in Bellingham, Massachusetts; died 26 October 1798 in Bellingham, Massachusetts.
460	ix.	Hannah Darling, born 09 April 1773 in Bellingham, Massachusetts. She married (1) Daniel Jones 30 June 1796 in Bellingham, Massachusetts. She married (2) Samuel Scott 25 June 1856 in Bellingham, Massachusetts; born 1770.
461	x.	Seth Darling, born 28 April 1777 in Bellingham, Massachusetts. He married (1) Susanna Cook 09 March 1800 in Bellingham, Massachusetts; born 1780. He married (2) Susanna Clark 02 January 1814 in Mendon, Massachusetts.
462	xi.	Uriah Darling, born 15 September 1781 in Bellingham, Massachusetts; died 27 August 1785 in Bellingham, Massachusetts.

140. Joshua[5] Darling (Samuel[4], Captain John[3], Denice[2], George[1]) was born 20 November 1739 in Bellingham, Massachusetts, and died 21 May 1815 in Bellingham, Massachusetts. He married **Martha Wilson** 26 February 1762 in Bellingham, Massachusetts, daughter of Robert Wilson and Martha. She was born 1732.

Children of Joshua Darling and Martha Wilson are:

	463	i.	Phila[6] Darling, born 27 March 1763 in Bellingham, Massachusetts. She married Jesse Sumner 25 November 1790 in Bellingham, Massachusetts.
+	464	ii.	Ahimaaz Darling, born 19 March 1765 in Bellingham, Massachusetts; died 30 October 1836 in Bellingham, Massachusetts.
	465	iii.	Abisha Darling, born 02 April 1767 in Bellingham, Massachusetts.

466	iv.	Amasa Darling, born 30 April 1769 in Bellingham, Massachusetts; died 19 November 1825 in Bellingham, Massachusetts.
467	v.	Patty Darling, born 29 November 1770 in Bellingham, Massachusetts. She married Darius Fisk 05 January 1789 in Bellingham, Massachusetts.
468	vi.	Michael Darling, born 20 February 1773 in Bellingham, Massachusetts; died 26 July 1795 in Bellingham, Massachusetts.
469	vii.	William Darling, born 30 September 1778 in Bellingham, Massachusetts; died 17 January 1810 in Bellingham, Massachusetts.

141. Penelope[5] Darling (Samuel[4], Captain John[3], Denice[2], George[1]) was born 25 August 1742 in Bellingham, Massachusetts. She married **Israel Wilson** 18 July 1765 in Bellingham, Massachusetts, son of Robert Wilson and Martha.

Children of Penelope Darling and Israel Wilson are:

	470	i.	Joseph[6] Wilson.
+	471	ii.	Benjamin Wilson.
	472	iii.	Israel Wilson, born 1768.

145. Jonathan[5] Draper (Mary[4] Darling, Captain John[3], Denice[2], George[1]) was born 10 May 1730 in Bellingham, Massachusetts. He married **Abigail Darling** 11 April 1753 in Bellingham, Massachusetts, daughter of Samuel Darling and Mary Thompson. She was born 16 February 1730/31 in Bellingham, Massachusetts, and died 23 June 1826 in Bellingham, Massachusetts.

Children are listed above under (136) Abigail Darling

154. Ichabod[5] Brown (Anna[4] Darling, Captain John[3], Denice[2], George[1]) was born 31 March 1711 in Rehoboth, Massachusetts. He married **Mary Darling** 09 September 1736 in Rehoboth, Massachusetts, daughter of John Darling and Hannah Staples. She was born 02 March 1711/12.

Child is listed above under (80) Mary Darling

160. Gideon[5] Brown (Anna[4] Darling, Captain John[3], Denice[2], George[1]) was born 10 December 1722.

Child of Gideon Brown is:

473   i.   Hannah[6] Brown, born 25 March 1756; died 28 November 1815. She married Daniel Sprague 07 January 1781 in Johnston, Rhode Island; born 10 July 1752 in Providence, Rhode Island; died 27 March 1816 in Smithfield, Rhode Island.

163. Enoch[5] Darling (David[4], Cornelius[3], Denice[2], George[1]) was born 29 September 1727 in Wrentham, Massachusetts, and died 10 September 1792 in Bellingham, Massachusetts. He married **Lois Thompson** 26 November 1751 in Smithfield, Rhode Island.

Children of Enoch Darling and Lois Thompson are:

474   i.   Lydia[6] Darling, born 11 January 1752 in Bellingham, Massachusetts. She married Ebenezer Hartshorn 06 July 1772 in Medway, Massachusetts.

475   ii.   Rachel Darling, born 09 December 1753 in Bellingham, Massachusetts.

476   iii. Elijah Darling, born 14 September 1756.

165. Timothy[5] Darling (David[4], Cornelius[3], Denice[2], George[1]) was born 14 April 1731 in Wrentham, Massachusetts, and died 1784 in Grafton, Massachusetts. He married **(1) Elizabeth Rice** 01 July 1756 in Grafton, Massachusetts, daughter of Phineas Rice and Elizabeth Willard. He married **(2) Abigail Leland** 28 July 1774 in Grafton, Massachusetts, daughter of James Leland and Mary Warren. She was born 23 May 1750 in Grafton, Massachusetts, and died 06 October 1803 in Sutton, Massachusetts.

Child of Timothy Darling and Elizabeth Rice is:

477   i.   John[6] Darling, born 1773 in Grafton, Massachusetts. He married Chloe Rideout.

Children of Timothy Darling and Abigail Leland are:

+   478   i.   Alden[6] Darling, born 1774; died 1844 in New York.

479   ii. Elizabeth Darling, born 1778 in Grafton, Massachusetts. She married Joseph Hall.

173. Job[5] Darling (Cornelius[4], Cornelius[3], Denice[2], George[1]) was born 02 January 1726/27 in Bellingham, Massachusetts, and died 26 March 1814 in Framingham, Massachusetts. He married **(1) Mary Ballou** 01 December 1756 in Bellingham, Massachusetts. He married **(2) Margery Cook** 15 March 1764 in Bellingham, Massachusetts, daughter of Walter Cook and Margery Corbett. She was born 18 August 1734 in Mendon, Massachusetts.

Child of Job Darling and Margery Cook is:

480   i.   Mary[6] Darling, born 23 December 1769 in Mendon, Massachusetts.

174. Cornelius[5] Darling (Cornelius[4], Cornelius[3], Denice[2], George[1]) was born 15 March 1731/32 in Bellingham, Massachusetts, and died 22 March 1816 in Bellingham, Massachusetts. He married **Mehitable Corbett**, daughter of Joseph Corbett and Deborah Albee. She was born 13 March 1740/41 in Mendon, Massachusetts, and died 15 March 1816 in Bellingham, Massachusetts.

Children of Cornelius Darling and Mehitable Corbett are:

+   481   i.   Phebe[6] Darling, born 18 March 1767 in Bellingham, Massachusetts; died 12 November 1861 in Bellingham, Massachusetts.

482   ii. Deborah Darling, born 22 December 1775 in Bellingham, Massachusetts.

181. Susannah[5] Martin (John[4], Hannah[3] Darling, Denice[2], George[1]),   She married **Benjamin Colman** 25 December 1775. He was born 03 August 1749 in Lunenburg, Massachusetts.

Child of Susannah Martin and Benjamin Colman is:
+   483   i.   Asenath[6] Colman, born 07 October 1776; died 04 December 1848.

182. Silas[5] Thayer (Abigail[4] Darling, Daniel[3], Denice[2], George[1]) was born 1731. He married **(1) Perley Pond** 20 August 1767 in Mendon, Massachusetts, daughter of John Pond and Mary. She was born 1750 in Mendon, Massachusetts. He married **(2) Rachel Hanks** 1790. She was born 1738 in Mendon, Massachusetts.

Children of Silas Thayer and Perley Pond are:
    484   i.   Charlotte[6] Thayer, born 19 February 1768 in Mendon, Massachusetts.
+   485   ii.   Jarvis Thayer, born 20 November 1770 in Mendon, Massachusetts; died January 1834.
    486   iii. Sabra Thayer, born 05 April 1772 in Mendon, Massachusetts.
    487   iv.   Olive Thayer, born 11 April 1774 in Mendon, Massachusett.
    488   v.   Simon Thayer, born 13 July 1778 in Mendon, Massachusetts.
    489   vi.   Mary Thayer, born 06 December 1782 in Mendon, Massachusetts.
    490   vii. Perley Thayer, born 18 January 1785 in Mendon, Massachusetts.
    491   viii. Rebecca Thayer, born 07 May 1787 in Mendon, Massachusetts.
    492   ix.   Silas Thayer, born 10 March 1789 in Mendon, Massachusetts; died 1836   He married Harriet Pearl; died 1829.
    493   x.   John Thayer, born 28 April 1791 in Mendon, Massachusetts. He married Sally A. Town 1822; born 13 November 1795 died 14 April 1854.
    494   xi.   Rachel Thayer, born 22 February 1792 in Mendon, Massachuset; died 06 October 1794 in Mendon, Massachusetts.

495	xii.	Rachel Thayer, born 04 December 1794 in Mendon, Massachusetts; died 02 October 1795 in Mendon, Massachusetts.
496	xiii.	Haddasha Thayer, born 13 July 1796 in Mendon, Massachusetts.
497	xiv.	Jemima Thayer, born 25 August 1798 in Mendon, Massachusetts.
+ 498	xv.	William H. Thayer, born 13 February 1801 in Mendon, Massachusetts; died 22 August 1844.
499	xvi.	Jacob Thayer, born in Mendon, Massachusetts; died 1828 in Long Island, New York.

186. Jesse⁵ Darling (Daniel⁴, Daniel³, Denice², George¹) was born 1743 in Mendon, Massachusetts, and died 09 July 1813 in Mendon, Massachusetts. He married **Hannah Southwick** 22 May 1771 in Mendon, Massachusetts. She was born 1750 in Mendon, Massachusetts, and died 19 April 1792 in Uxbridge, Massachusetts.

Notes for Jesse Darling:
Jesse Darling and his wife Hannah Southwick are buried at the Blackstone Cemetery, located on Mendon Street in Blackstone, Massachuusetts

Children of Jesse Darling and Hannah Southwick are:

500	i.	Elathan⁶ Darling, born 30 April 1773 in Mendon, Massachusetts; died 10 August 1793 in Mendon, Massachusetts.
501	ii.	James Darling, born 1779 in Mendon, Massachusetts; died 06 May 1804 in Mendon, Massachusetts.

> Notes for James Darling
> James Darling is also buried at the Blackstone Cemetery

187. Matthew⁵ Darling (Daniel⁴, Daniel³, Denice², George¹) was born 1745 in Mendon, Massachusetts. He married **Hannah Emerson**.

Children of Matthew Darling and Hannah Emerson are:

502	i.	Olive[6] Darling, born 20 November 1768 in Mendon, Massachusetts; died 20 May 1772 in Mendon, Massachusetts.
503	ii.	Bethany Darling, born 17 February 1771 in Mendon, Massachusetts; died 17 March 1777 in Mendon, Massachusetts.
504	iii.	Phebe Darling, born 01 August 1774 in Mendon, Massachusetts; died 09 March 1777 in Mendon, Massachusetts.
505	iv.	Olive Darling, born 23 June 1776 in Mendon, Massachusetts.
506	v.	Daniel Darling, born 01 April 1779 in Mendon, Massachusetts.
507	vi.	Sarah Darling, born 21 May 1786 in Mendon, Massachusetts.
508	vii.	Mary Darling, born 08 September 1792 in Mendon, Massachusetts.

188. Mary[5] Darling (Daniel[4], Daniel[3], Denice[2], George[1]) was born 04 September 1752 in Mendon, Massachusetts, and died 24 December 1841. She married **Jonathan Emerson** 21 November 1774, son of Jonathan Emerson and Sarah Marshall. He was born 25 February 1754, and died 27 April 1842.

Children of Mary Darling and Jonathan Emerson are:

509	i.	Samuel[6] Emerson, born 20 July 1776 in Uxbridge, Massachusetts; died 29 October 1860. He married Eunice Whipple 23 January 1803; born 01 December 1780 in Uxbridge, Massachusetts.
510	ii.	Waitstill Emerson, born 04 January 1780. She married Howard Wood 25 April 1804.
511	iii.	Lydia Emerson, born 14 February 1784 in Uxbridge, Massachusetts. She married Richard Arnold 09 April 1809.

191. Job[5] Darling (Samuel[4], Daniel[3], Denice[2], George[1]) was born 1749 in Mendon, Massachusetts, and died 27 November 1836 in Sutton, Massachusetts. He married **(1) Margery Cook** 14 March 1764 in Mendon, Massachusetts, daughter of Walter Cook and Margery Corbett. She was born 1750. He married **(2) Abigail Pegsley** 16 July 1775.

Children of Job Darling and Margery Cook are:

512   i.   Huldah[6] Darling, born 16 June 1765 in Bellingham, Massachusetts; died 26 November 1765 in Bellingham, Massachusetts.

513   ii. Huldah Darling, born 11 September 1766 in Bellingham, Massachusetts. She married Timothy Merriam 30 June 1785 in Cumberland, Rhode Island.

514   iii. Caleb Darling, born 05 September 1768 in Mendon, Massachusetts; died 13 August 1853 in Framingham, Massachusetts.

515   iv. Mary Darling, born 23 December 1769 in Mendon, Massachusetts.

516   v.   Hannah Darling, born 09 October 1772 in Mendon, Massachusetts.

Child of Job Darling and Abigail Pegsley is:

+   517   i.   Elisha[6] Darling, born 1776; died 10 July 1858 in Burrillville, Rhode Island.

195. David[5] Darling (Samuel[4], Daniel[3], Denice[2], George[1]) was born 21 October 1760 in Mendon, Massachusetts, and died 24 August 1829 in New York. He married **(1) Elizabeth Goldthwaite** 05 February 1784 in Mendon, Massachusetts. He married **(2) Massa Phillips** 04 June 1791 in Glocester, Rhode Island. She was born 12 February 1771 in Glocester, Rhode Island, and died 02 July 1853.

Children of David Darling and Massa Phillips are:

518   i.   Joshua[6] Darling.

519   ii. Darius Darling, born 20 October 1793. He married (1) Eliza Ann Pierce. He married (2) Sally Albee 1816.

520   iii. Ruth Darling, born 12 February 1796. She married (1) Charles Henry Webb. She married (2) Hiram Coe.

521   iv. Artemus Darling, born 21 April 1807; died 14 December 1884 in New York. He married Lorinda Taft 05 November 1826 in Mendon, Massachusetts; born 14 February 1802 in Mendon, Massachusetts.

              Notes for Lorinda Taft:
              Lorinda Taft Darling is also buried at the Swan Point Cemetery

522	v.	Mercy Darling, born 20 April 1803. She married Dexter Hunt.
523	vi.	David Darling, born 20 May 1805.
524	vii.	Stephen Darling, born 25 April 1807.

198. Benson[5] Darling (Samuel[4], Daniel[3], Denice[2], George[1]) was born 1772 in Mendon, Massachusetts, and died 23 February 1842 in Mendon, Massachusetts. He married **(1) Lusina Washburn**. He married **(2) Lois Albee** 29 November 1798 in Mendon, Massachusetts, daughter of Stephen Albee and Mary Wood. She was born 05 May 1766 in Mendon, Massachusetts.

Children of Benson Darling and Lois Albee are:

	525	i.	Urania[6] Darling, born 14 April 1799 in Mendon, Massachusetts. She married Atwood Cady 18 August 1822 in Mendon, Massachusetts.
	526	ii.	Samuel Darling, born 18 December 1801 in Mendon, Massachusetts. He married Sylvia Taft 10 October 1820 in Mendon, Massachusetts; born 27 September 1803 in Mendon, Massachusetts.
+	527	iii.	Lyman Darling, born 08 February 1803 in Mendon, Massachusetts; died 18 October 1873 in Mendon, Massachusetts.
+	528	iv.	Artemus Darling, born 07 April 1798 in Mendon, Massachusetts; died 19 April 1861 in Providence, Rhode Island.
	529	v.	Seth Darling, born 1811 in Mendon, Massachusetts; died 1838 in Mendon, Massachusetts.
	530	vi.	Warren Darling, born 1815 in Mendon, Massachusetts; died 29 September 1887 in Cranston, Rhode Island. He married (1) Anna Roil. He married (2) Sylvia Taft 16 May 1842.

207. Jemima[5] Thompson (Susannah[4] Darling, Daniel[3], Denice[2], George[1]) was born 1755. She married **Phineas Taft**.

Children of Jemima Thompson and Phineas Taft are:

+	531	i.	Mary Susan[6] Taft, born 1781 in Danby, Vermont; died 1862.

211. Keziah[5] Hunt (Kezia[4] Darling, Daniel[3], Denice[2], George[1]) was born 1745. She married **Daniel Wheelock**, son of Daniel Wheelock and Deborah Darling. He was born 13 August 1744.

Child of Keziah Hunt and Daniel Wheelock is:

533	i.	Hannah[6] Wheelock.

214. Peter[5] Hunt (Kezia[4] Darling, Daniel[3], Denice[2], George[1]) was born 1753.

Child of Peter Hunt is:

+	534	i.	Sarah[6] Hunt, died 28 January 1892.

218. Zeleck[5] Darling (William[4], Daniel[3], Denice[2], George[1]) was born 05 June 1762 in Mendon, Massachusetts, and died 28 January 1844 in Sutton, Massachusetts. He married **(1) Sarah Blake** 27 November 1785 in Mendon, Massachusetts. She was born 1752. He married **(2) Polly Elliot** 02 August 1812 in Sutton, Massachusetts. She was born 1784, and died 26 January 1843 in Sutton, Massachusetts.

Children of Zeleck Darling and Sarah Blake are:

+	535	i.	Cyrus[6] Darling, born 01 September 1787 in Sutton, Massachusetts.
+	536	ii.	Wheeler Darling, born 19 November 1789 in Sutton, Massachusetts.
	537	iii.	Peter Darling, born 07 January 1792 in Sutton, Massachusetts.
+	538	iv.	Zelek Darling, born 16 February 1794 in Sutton, Massachusetts.
	539	v.	Simeon Darling, born 13 April 1796 in Sutton, Massachusetts.
	540	vi.	John Darling, born 09 December 1798 in Sutton, Massachusetts.
	541	vii.	Levi Darling, born 03 November 1800 in Sutton, Massachusetts.

Children of Zeleck Darling and Polly Elliot are:

542   i.   Moses Leland[6] Darling, born 07 November 1812 in Sutton, Massachusetts.

543   ii.   Harrison Darling, born 15 July 1814 in Sutton, Massachusetts.

544   iii. Lydia Darling, born 21 October 1816 in Sutton, Massachusetts.

545   iv. Ruth Darling, born 21 September 1818 in Sutton, Massachusetts.

546   v.   Fuller Darling, born 24 March 1821 in Sutton, Massachusetts.

547   vi. Palmer Darling, born 16 May 1823 in Sutton, Massachusetts.

548   vii. Judson Darling, born 05 May 1827 in Sutton, Massachusetts.

220. Ehud[5] Darling (William[4], Daniel[3], Denice[2], George[1]) was born 1768 in Mendon, Massachusetts, and died in New York. He married **Patty Tyler** 01 March 1793 in Sutton, Massachusetts.

Children of Ehud Darling and Patty Tyler are:

549   i.   Roxanna[6] Darling, born November 1795.

550   ii.   Elizabeth Darling, born October 1796.

551   iii. Martha Darling, born 1802.

552   iv. Socrates Darling, born 24 April 1804; died 06 April 1870 in Texas. He married (1) Julia Ann Woodward. He married (2) Lorraine Jones.

553   v.   Rebecca Darling, born 1807.

554   vi. Horace Darling, born 1809.

555   vii. Horatio Nelson Darling, born 1811.

556   viii. Isaac Darling, born 1813.

557   ix. Ransom Darling, born 1815.

558   x.   William Darling, born 29 July 1819; died 21 January 1901 in New York. He married Luduska Aldrich.

559   xi. Alva Darling, born 1821; died in INFANCY.

222. Aaron[5] Darling (William[4], Daniel[3], Denice[2], George[1]) was born 1771 in Mendon, Massachusetts, and died 24 January 1849. He married **Mercy Pratt** 26 August 1794 in Sutton, Massachusetts. She was born 1777 in Smithfield, Rhode Island.

Child of Aaron Darling and Mercy Pratt is:

560   i.   Freelove[6] Darling, born 1808; died 1853.

225. William[5] Darling (William[4], Daniel[3], Denice[2], George[1]) was born 1776 in Mendon, Massachusetts. He married **Permilla Cox** 28 August 1803 in Sutton, Massachusetts.

Children of William Darling and Permilla Cox are:

561   i.   Elmira[6] Darling, born 01 February 1804 in Sutton, Massachusetts.

562   ii.   Stephen Darling, born 16 February 1805 in Sutton, Massachusetts.

563   iii.   Mary Ann Darling, born 30 September 1806 in Sutton, Massachusetts.

564   iv.   Philander Darling, born 19 August 1808 in Sutton, Massachusetts. He married Rhoda Young 18 November 1832 in Mendon, Massachusetts.

565   v.   Marcia Darling, born 25 December 1810 in Sutton, Massachusetts.

566   vi.   Eli Darling, born 09 January 1813 in Sutton, Massachusetts.

567   vii.   John Darling, born 16 November 1814 in Sutton, Massachusetts.

568   viii.   Sarah Ann Darling, born 16 August 1816 in Sutton, Massachusetts.

569   ix.   Gardner Darling, born 10 March 1819 in Sutton, Massachusetts.

570   x.   Jane Frances Darling, born 09 February 1821 in Sutton, Massachusetts.

571   xi.   Louisa Darling, born 12 May 1823 in Sutton, Massachusetts.

572   xii.   William Gardner Darling, born 12 May 1825 in Sutton, Massachusetts.

573   xiii.   Permilla Darling, born 30 April 1827 in Sutton, Massachusetts.

574   xiv.   Prudence Darling, born 30 April 1827 in Sutton, Massachusetts.

228. Elias[5] Wheelock (Obadiah[4], Elizabeth[3] Darling, Denice[2], George[1]) was born 17 April 1743 in Mendon, Massachusetts, and died 1821. He married **Sarah Rice**, daughter of Beriah Rice and Mary Goodenow. She was born 16 August 1751.

Child of Elias Wheelock and Sarah Rice is:
    575   i.   Amoret[6] Wheelock.

233. Bathsheba[5] Wheelock (Josiah[4], Elizabeth[3] Darling, Denice[2], George[1]) was born 14 December 1760 in Mendon, Massachusetts, and died 04 November 1816. She married **Jotham Thayer** 29 August 1784, son of Seth Thayer and Judith Bullard. He was born 12 February 1761 in Mendon, Massachusetts, and died 18 March 1825 in Milford, Massachusetts.

Notes for Bathsheba Wheelock:
Bathsheba Wheelock is buried at the South Hopedale Cemetery, located on Plain Street in Hopedale, Massachusetts

Notes for Jotham Thayer:
He is buried at the South Hopedale Cemetery, located on Plain Street in Hopedale, Massachusetts

Children of Bathsheba Wheelock and Jotham Thayer are:
    576   i.   Alexander[6] Thayer, born 07 October 1785 in Milford, Massachusetts; died 1825.
    577   ii.   Experience Thayer, born 20 July 1786 in Milford, Massachusetts.
    578   iii. Lucretia Thayer, born 29 July 1787 in Milford, Massachusetts.
    579   iv.   Dency Thayer, born 24 May 1805 in Milford, Massachusetts She married (1) Darius Daniels Farnham[7] 06 July 1820; born 19 November 1798 in Uxbridge, Massachusetts. She married (2) Estus Lamb 09 June 1842; born 1801.

248. Paul[5] Wheelock (Deborah[4] Darling, Benjamin[3], Denice[2], George[1]) was born 09 February 1736/37 in Uxbridge, Massachusetts. He married **Lydia Sayles**.

Child of Paul Wheelock and Lydia Sayles is:
 + 580   i.   Rowena[6] Wheelock, born 20 December 1760 in of Uxbridge, Massachusetts; died 1802.

250. Daniel[5] Wheelock (Deborah[4] Darling, Benjamin[3], Denice[2], George[1]) was born 13 August 1744. He married **Keziah Hunt**, daughter of John Hunt and Kezia Darling. She was born 1745.

Child is listed above under (211) Keziah Hunt.

261. Joseph[5] Darling (Joseph[4], Benjamin[3], Denice[2], George[1]) was born 06 April 1736 in Mendon, Massachusetts. He married **(1) Sarah Thayer.** He married **(2) Jerusha Thayer** February 1760 in Mendon, Massachusetts, daughter of Ebenezer Thayer and Sarah. She was born 26 March 1740 in Mendon, Massachusetts.

Child of Joseph Darling and Sarah Thayer is:

581	i.	Levi[6] Darling, born 28 December 1757 in Mendon, Massachusetts.

Children of Joseph Darling and Jerusha Thayer are:

+ 582	i.	Jerusha[6] Darling, born 15 March 1761 in Mendon, Massachusetts.
583	ii.	Ichabod Darling, born 01 June 1764 in Mendon, Massachusetts.

262. Stephen[5] Darling (Joseph[4], Benjamin[3], Denice[2], George[1]) was born 21 August 1738 in Mendon, Massachusetts, and died in Richmond, New Hampshire. He married **(1) Prudence White** 25 December 1760 in Mendon, Massachusetts, daughter of Aaron White and Susanna Benson. She was born 1739 in Mendon, Massachusetts, and died 12 April 1799 in Richmond, New Hampshire. He married **(2) Elizabeth Scott** 25 December 1799 in Richmond, New Hampshire.

Children of Stephen Darling and Prudence White are:

584	i.	Chloe[6] Darling, born 10 May 1769. She married Luke Scott 30 November 1786; born 11 May 1765 in Vermont.
585	ii.	Lucy Darling, born 05 August 1773 in Mendon, Massachusetts; died 09 March 1848 in Pennsylvania. She married Charles Carpenter; born 30 September 1768 in Rehoboth, Massachusetts.

Children of Stephen Darling and Elizabeth Scott are:

586   i.   Luke[6] Darling, born 19 March 1806.
587   ii. Prudence Darling.

263. Lydia[5] Darling (Joseph[4], Benjamin[3], Denice[2], George[1]) was born 21 April 1743 in Mendon, Massachusetts, and died 12 July 1807 in New Hampshire. She married **Peter Holbrook**. He was born 03 May 1740 in Uxbridge, Massachusetts.

Children of Lydia Darling and Peter Holbrook are:

588   i.   Eunice[6] Holbrook, born 1762. She married Ivory Snow, born 1758.
589   ii.   Joseph Holbrook, born 1762. He married Lucinda Cook; born 1769.
590   iii. Mary Holbrook, born 18 March 1768. She married Nathan Ballou; born 09 September 1760.
591   iv.   Peter Holbrook, born 1770.
592   v.   Stephen Holbrook, born 23 May 1775. He married Mary Whitcomb; born 1784.
593   vi.   Henry Holbrook, born 24 May 1777. He married Joanna Taft; born 1781.
594   vii. Lydia Holbrook, born 03 September 1779.
595   viii. Abigail Holbrook, born 01 September 1781. She married Nathan Hex; born 1777.
596   ix.   Samuel Holbrook, born 17 August 1784. He married Polly Crosett; born 1785.
597   x.   Rachel Holbrook, born 09 October 1786. She married Thomas Prime; born 1782.

264. Enoch[5] Darling (Joseph[4], Benjamin[3], Denice[2], George[1]) was born 08 July 1746 in Mendon, Massachusetts. He married **(1) Elizabeth Harper** 19 June 1768 in Mendon, Massachusetts. She was born 1750 in Mendon, Massachusetts. He married **(2) Lois Garnsey** 09 July 1779 in Mendon, Massachusetts. She was born 05 July 1758 in Rehoboth, Massachusetts.

Child of Enoch Darling and Elizabeth Harper is:

598   i.   Nancy[6] Darling, born 15 February 1769 in Mendon, Massachusetts.

Children of Enoch Darling and Lois Garnsey are:
599   i.   Charlotte[6] Darling, born 14 September 1768 in Bellingham, Massachusetts.
600   ii.   Elijah Darling, born 14 September 1756 in Bellingham, Massachusetts.
601   iii.   Eunice Darling, born 11 August 1758 in Bellingham, Massachusetts.

267. Jacob[5] Darling (Joseph[4], Benjamin[3], Denice[2], George[1]) was born 02 December 1751 in Mendon, Massachusetts, and died 01 February 1822 in Indiana. He married **Sarah Cutler** 30 September 1779 in Falmouth, Massachusetts. She was born 26 July 1763 in Falmouth, Massachusetts, and died 28 December 1846 in Indiana.

Children of Jacob Darling and Sarah Cutler are:
+   602   i.   Thomas Jefferson[6] Darling, born 1784 in Hebron, New York; died 1865 in Indiana.
      603   ii.   Elijah Darling, born 1786 in New York. He married Charlotte Tower 17 October 1808 in New York; born 20 January 1791 in Attleboro, Massachusetts; died 29 April 1875.
+   604   iii.   James C. Darling, born 1786 in New York.
      605   iv.   Sarah Darling, born 22 May 1788 in New York; died 23 May 1865. She married John Palmer; born 30 April 1781; died 20 March 1843 in Indiana.
      606   v.   Jacob Darling, born 1790.
      607   vi.   Irene Darling, born 02 August 1781; died 04 October 1849. She married Joseph Baker; born 1787.
      608   vii.   Polly Darling, born 1793. She married George Beach; born 1789.
      609 viii.   John Russell Darling, born 18 April 1804 in New York; died 25 November 1872 in Indiana. He married Ann Gibson 18 January 1827; born 04 January 1808.
      610   ix.   Dorcas Darling, born 1809 in New York.

268. David⁵ Darling (Ebenezer⁴, Benjamin³, Denice²,
George¹) was born 1747 in Glocester, Rhode Island, and died 1823
in North Adams, Massachusetts. He married **Melia
Veazey/Amelia Veazie** 10 April 1767 in Glocester, Rhode Island.
She was born 1748 in Glocester, Rhode Island.

Children of David Darling and Melia Veazie are:

+   611   i.   David⁶ Darling, born 12 January 1768 in Glocester, Rhode
                  Island; died 25 October 1846 in North Adams,
                  Massachusetts.
     612   ii.   Thankful Darling, born 1771.

269. Andrew⁵ Darling (Ebenezer⁴, Benjamin³, Denice²,
George¹) was born 22 May 1749 in Glocester, Rhode Island, and
died 02 August 1790 in Burrillville, Rhode Island. He married
Sarah Potter 07 November 1773 in Glocester, Rhode Island,
daughter of Abiel Potter. She was born 1752 in Glocester, Rhode
Island.

Children of Andrew Darling and Sarah Potter are:

     613   i.   Thomas⁶ Darling, born in Glocester, Rhode Island. He
                  married Sarah Steere 02 August 1807 in Burrillville, Rhode
                  Island.
     614   ii.   Hopey Darling, born 1775 in Glocester, Rhode Island.
     615   iii. Lucretia Darling, born 1787 in Glocester, Rhode Island. She
                  married Joseph Ballou 30 August 1801 in Glocester, Rhode
                  Island; born 30 October 1783 in Glocester, Rhode Island.
     616   iv.   Silencey Darling.
     617   v.   Sarah Darling, born in Burrillville, Rhode Island. She
                  married Daniel Mathewson.
     618   vi.   Mary Darling, born in Burrillville, Rhode Island. She
                  married Arca Walling 21 March 1813 in Glocester, Rhode
                  Island.
     619   vii. Lydia Darling, born 08 April 1785 in Glocester, Rhode
                  Island; died 06 April 1857. She married (1) Darling
                  Mathewson. She married (2) Albert Mathewson 01 July
                  1798 in Glocester, Rhode Island.
+   620   viii. Andrew Darling, born 1790 in Burrillville, Rhode Island.

271. Ebenezer⁵ Darling (Ebenezer⁴, Benjamin³, Denice², George¹) was born June 1751 in Glocester, Rhode Island, and died December 1820 in Glocester, Rhode Island. He married **Lydia Bowen** 1775, daughter of Eleazer Bowen and Lydia Wood. She was born 1752, and died 17 February 1833 in Glocester, Rhode Island.

Children of Ebenezer Darling and Lydia Bowen are:

621	i.	Andrew⁶ Darling, born 1779 in Chepachet, Rhode Island.
+ 622	ii.	Darius Darling, born 1781 in Glocester, Rhode Island; died 14 December 1861 in Glocester, Rhode Island.
+ 623	iii.	William Darling, born December 1777 in Glocester, Rhode Island; died 01 July 1811 in Glocester, Rhode Island.
624	iv.	Lydia Darling, born 1789; died 08 December 1810. She married Charles Underwood 08 December 1808 in Glocester, Rhode Island.
625	v.	Mary Darling, born April 1791; died 14 December 1820 in Glocester, Rhode Island. She married James Sprague; born 09 September 1782 in Glocester, Rhode Island.

272. Dorcas⁵ Darling (Ebenezer⁴, Benjamin³, Denice², George¹) was born 09 July 1759 in Glocester, Rhode Island, and died 16 September 1852 in Glocester, Rhode Island. She married **Jeremiah Sweet** 13 March 1780 in Glocester, Rhode Island. He was born 03 February 1757 in Glocester, Rhode Island.

Children of Dorcas Darling and Jeremiah Sweet are:

626	i.	Timothy⁶ Sweet, born 19 January 1781 in Glocester, Rhode Island; died 17 March 1845 in Glocester, Rhode Island. He married Abigail Page 29 May 1803 in Glocester, Rhode Island; born 07 August 1782.
627	ii.	Mary Sweet. She married Darius Durfrey.
628	iii.	Anna Sweet, born 1782; died 06 November 1862 in Glocester, Rhode Island. She married Thomas Peckham; born 10 January 1780.
629	iv.	Dorcas Sweet.
630	v.	Elizabeth Sweet.
631	vi.	Esther Sweet, born 1795; died 17 September 1824 in Glocester, Rhode Island.

275. Martha^5 Darling (Ebenezer^4, Benjamin^3, Denice^2, George^1) was born 1765 in Glocester, Rhode Island, and died 1847 in Glocester, Rhode Island. She married **James Bowen**, son of Eleazer Bowen and Lydia Wood. He was born 12 December 1759 in Glocester, Rhode Island, and died 29 August 1850 in Glocester, Rhode Island.

Notes for Martha Darling
Martha Darling is buried at the Rhode Island Historical Cemetery #71

Children of Martha Darling and James Bowen are:

632	i.	Candace^6 Bowen.
633	ii.	Rhoda Bowen.
634	iii.	Martin Bowen.

280. Peter^5 Darling (Peter^4, Benjamin^3, Denice^2, George^1) was born 22 August 1757 in Cumberland, Rhode Island, and died 13 November 1796 in Cumberland, Rhode Island. He married **Jerusha Darling** 01 January 1778 in Cumberland, Rhode Island, daughter of Joseph Darling and Jerusha Thayer. She was born 15 March 1761 in Mendon, Massachusetts.

Children of Peter Darling and Jerusha Darling are:

635	i.	Nathan^6 Darling, born 07 August 1779 in Cumberland, Rhode Island.
636	ii.	Precilla Darling, born 24 May 1781 in Cumberland, Rhode Island; died 1798 in Cumberland, Rhode Island.
637	iii.	Amey Darling, born 20 July 1784 in Cumberland, Rhode Island.
638	iv.	Anna Darling, born 05 October 1790 in Cumberland, Rhode Island.
639	v.	Jerusha Darling, born 14 June 1793 in Cumberland, Rhode Island; died 1795 in Cumberland, Rhode Island.
640	vi.	Peter Darling, born 10 May 1795 in Cumberland, Rhode Island.
641	vii.	Elihue Darling.

281. Darius[5] Darling (Peter[4], Benjamin[3], Denice[2], George[1]) was born 21 May 1769 in Cumberland, Rhode Island. He married **Amey**.

Children of Darius Darling and Amey are:

642	i.	Anson[6] Darling, born 14 February 1798 in Cumberland, Rhode Island.
643	ii.	Nancy Darling, born 02 September 1801.

285. Welcome[5] Darling (Peter[4], Benjamin[3], Denice[2], George[1]) was born in Cumberland, Rhode Island. He married **Sarah Goodale** 18 March 1810 in Cumberland, Rhode Island.

Children of Welcome Darling and Sarah Goodale are:

+	644	i.	Welcome Greene[6] Darling, born 29 October 1810 in Cumberland, Rhode Island; died 26 April 1870 in Woonsocket, Rhode Island.
	645	ii.	Almon Darling, born 02 January 1812 in Cumberland, Rhode Island.
	646	iii.	William Loring Darling, born 17 June 1823 in Cumberland, Rhode Island; died 10 December 1854 in Cumberland, Rhode Island.

287. Benjamin[5] Darling (Peter[4], Benjamin[3], Denice[2], George[1]) was born 23 July 1774 in Cumberland, Rhode Island. He married **Lavina Jillson** 18 November 1798 in Cumberland, Rhode Island, daughter of Nathan Jillson and Susannah Sheldon. She was born 1779 in Cumberland, Rhode Island, and died 19 September 1834 in Cumberland, Rhode Island.

Children of Benjamin Darling and Lavina Jillson are:

647	i.	Barton[6] Darling, born 31 July 1799 in Cumberland, Rhode Island; died 06 July 1848.
648	ii.	Newton Darling, born 14 February 1802 in Cumberland, Rhode Island; died 04 August 1803 in Cumberland, Rhode Island.
649	iii.	Alvin Darling, born 16 May 1804 in Cumberland, Rhode Island; died 11 May 1856 }

650	iv.	Susan Darling, born 06 January 1807 in Cumberland, Rhode Island.
651	v.	Benjamin M. Darling, born 29 September 1809 in Cumberland, Rhode Island.
652	vi.	Eliza Darling, born 08 October 1812 in Cumberland, Rhode Island; died 23 December 1818 in Cumberland, Rhode Island.
653	vii.	William P. Darling, born 07 August 1816 in Cumberland, Rhode Island.

289. Reuben[5] Darling (Peter[4], Benjamin[3], Denice[2], George[1]) was born December 1779 in Cumberland, Rhode Island, and died 04 July 1869. He married **Uranah Ballou** 15 November 1807 in Cumberland, Rhode Island, daughter of Duty Ballou and Waitstill Jillson. She was born 16 November 1780 in Cumberland, Rhode Island, and died 02 November 1848 in Woonsocket, Rhode Island.

Child of Reuben Darling and Uranah Ballou is:

654	i.	Warren[6] Darling, born 26 November 1809 in Cumberland, Rhode Island.

305. Lucy[5] Darling (Samuel[4], Benjamin[3], Denice[2], George[1]) was born 15 August 1772 in Bellingham, Massachusetts, and died 1830. She married **Whipple Cook** 10 November 1796 in Cumberland, Rhode Island, son of Nathaniel Cook and Amey Whipple. He was born 23 May 1773 in Cumberland, Rhode Island, and died 04 December 1858.

Children of Lucy Darling and Whipple Cook are:

655	i.	Alfred[6] Cook, born 1797, died 17 December 1840. He married Vienna Cook 20 February 1825 in Bellingham, Massachusetts; born 1867 in Pawtucket, Rhode Island.
656	ii.	Miranda Cook, born 18 April 1799. She married Thomas Thain 05 June 1826.
657	iii.	Winslow Cook, born 11 February 1801 in Franklin, Massachusetts. He married Lydia Tower 02 June 1861.

658	iv.	Whipple Cook, born 09 November 1802. He married Lucina Comstock
659	v.	Betsey Cook, born 05 October 1804. She married Nathan Comstock 07 May 1829.
660	vi.	Lucy Cook, born 09 June 1806. She married Benjamin W. Ripley 07 May 1829.
661	vii.	Maxcy Cook, born 03 June 1808. He married Ann Constock.
662	viii.	Charles M. Cook, born 09 April 1810; died 1831
663	ix.	Milton Coo born 12 June 1812. He married Louisa A. Cook 1841.
664	x.	Elbridge Gerry Cook, born 19 August 1815. He married Joanna Wilkinson 1842
665	xi.	Maria Cook, born 01 August 1819. She married John Butman.

308. Peter[5] Darling (Samuel[4], Benjamin[3], Denice[2], George[1])
was born 20 January 1752 in Mendon, Massachusetts, and died
June 1822 in Rowe, Massachusetts. He married **Sybil Thayer** 24
June 1776 in Uxbridge, Massachusetts.

Children of Peter Darling and Sybil Thayer are:

666	i.	Moses[6] Darling, born 17 August 1776 in Uxbridge, Massachusetts; died 23 September 1820 in Rowe, Massachusetts. He married Eunice Goodenough 22 August 1799.
667	ii.	Eunice Darling, born 1778.
668	iii.	Chloe Darling, born 1780.
669	iv.	Lydia Darling, born 11 April 1784.
670	v.	Rachel Darling, born 04 October 1792.
671	vi.	Peter Darling, born 05 March 1794.
672	vii.	Sally Darling, born 10 February 1800.

312. Henry[5] Darling (Samuel[4], Benjamin[3], Denice[2], George[1])
was born 03 July 1762 in Mendon, Massachusetts. He married **(1)**
Olive Herendeen 23 January 1784 in Smithfield, Rhode Island,
daughter of Hezekiah Herendeen and Freelove. She was born 06
February 1765 in Smithfield, Rhode Island. He married **(2)**
Mercy Alverson 05 February 1807 in Smithfield, Rhode Island,

daughter of Uriah Alverson and Nancy Sayles. She was born 1775.

Child of Henry Darling and Olive Herendeen is:

+ 673   i.   Henry[6] Darling, born 20 March 1784 in Smithfield, Rhode Island.

Children of Henry Darling and Mercy Alverson are:

674   i.   Sarah[6] Darling, born 12 September 1816 in Smithfield, Rhode Island.

675   ii.   Lewis Darling, born 17 June 1818 in Smithfield, Rhode Island.

313. Caleb[5] Darling (Samuel[4], Benjamin[3], Denice[2], George[1]) was born 30 November 1748 in Mendon, Massachusetts. He married **Sarah Albee** 13 February 1771 in Mendon, Massachusetts. She was born 1750.

Child of Caleb Darling and Sarah Albee is:

676   i.   Limon[6] Darling.

325. Joanna[5] Darling (Thomas[4], Benjamin[3], Denice[2], George[1]) was born 01 February 1752 in Mendon, Massachusetts. She married **Stephen Hilyard** 13 April 1769 in Mendon, Massachusetts. He was born 1747 in Mendon, Massachusetts.

Child of Joanna Darling and Stephen Hilyard is:

677   i.   Rhoda[6] Hilyard, born 15 January 1770 in Mendon, Massachusetts.

326. Rachel[5] Darling (Thomas[4], Benjamin[3], Denice[2], George[1)]) was born 01 May 1754 in Mendon, Massachusetts. She married **Reuben Holbrook** 27 March 1777 in Mendon, Massachusetts, son of Benjamin Holbrook and Abigail Benson.

He was born 18 July 1754 in Mendon, Massachusetts, and died 1835 in South Apalachin, New York.

More About Reuben Holbrook:
Reuben Holbrook served in the Revolutionary War

Children of Rachel Darling and Reuben Holbrook are:

678	i.	Darling[6] Holbrook.
679	ii.	Abigail Holbrook, born 08 January 1778 in Mendon, Massachusetts; died in Franklin, Bradford County, Pennsylvania. She married Leonard McKee ca.1798 in South Apalachin, New York.
680	iii.	Rachel Holbrook, born 08 January 1780 in Mendon, Massachusetts.
681	iv.	Prudence Holbrook born 25 February 1782 in Mendon, Massachusetts.
682	v.	Anna Holbrook, born 1785 in Mendon, Massachusetts.
683	vi.	Benjamin Holbrook, born 31 January 1786 in Mendon, Massachusetts.

328. Seth[5] Darling (Thomas[4], Benjamin[3], Denice[2], George[1]) was born 21 March 1760 in Mendon, Massachusetts, and died 27 March 1825 in Vermont. He married **Chloe Marsh** 06 October 1786 in Mendon, Massachusetts, daughter of Joseph Marsh and Deborah Staples. She was born 30 April 1768 in Mendon, Massachusetts, and died 21 October 1838 in Vermont.

Children of Seth Darling and Chloe Marsh are:

684	i.	Smith[6] Darling, born 02 December 1787 in Vermont; died 08 October 1871 in Smithfield, Rhode Island. He married Salome Wells 31 January 1814; born 01 May 1790 in New York.
685	ii.	Prudence Darling, born 1789 in Vermont.
686	iii.	Chloe Darling, born 1791 in Vermont.
687	iv.	Seth Darling, born 1794; died 1813.
688	v.	Jason Darling, born 04 April 1796 in Vermont; died 07 February 1864 in Vermont. He married Nancy Marsh 12 March 1822 in Vermont; born 13 March 1800.
689	vi.	Horace Darling, born 1798 in Vermont.
690	vii.	George Darling, born 1800 in Vermont.

691	viii.	Lewis Darling, born 05 March 1804 in Vermont; died 23 July 1882 in Pennsylvania. He married Lucy.
692	ix.	Jefferson Darling, born 1806 in Vermont.
693	x.	Madison Darling, born 1810 in Vermont.
694	xi.	Charles Darling, born 1812 in Vermont.

329. Simeon^5 Darling (Thomas^4, Benjamin^3, Denice^2, George^1) was born 21 March 1764 in Mendon, Massachusetts. He married **Anna Phelps** 24 June 1784 in Mendon, Massachusetts. She was born 1764.

Child of Simeon Darling and Anna Phelps is:

| + | 695 | i. | Thomas^6 Darling, born 21 June 1785 in Mendon, Massachusetts; died 15 November 1870 in Indiana. |

331. John^5 Darling (Thomas^4, Benjamin^3, Denice^2, George^1) was born 09 June 1768 in Mendon, Massachusetts. He married **Mary/Polly Warfield** 23 June 1790 in Mendon, Massachusetts. She was born 1768.

Children of John Darling and Mary/Polly Warfield are:

696	i.	John^6 Darling, born 12 November 1794. He married Laura Anderson.
697	ii.	Edward Darling, born 27 March 1797.
698	iii.	Leonard Darling, born 15 May 1799.

332. Nathan^5 Darling (Thomas^4, Benjamin^3, Denice^2, George^1) was born 17 December 1770 in Mendon, Massachusetts, and died 07 September 1855 in Hopedale, Massachusetts. He married **Polly Young** 06 April 1794 in Mendon, Massachusetts, daughter of Levi Young and Deborah Battles. She was born 09 December 1774 in Smithfield, Rhode Island, and died 25 May 1846 in Uxbridge, Massachusetts.

Children of Nathan Darling and Polly Young are:

| 699 | i. | Susan^6 Darling, born 18 June 1794 in Mendon, Massachusetts; died 1824. She married Samuel Taft 27 December 1812; born in Mendon, Massachusetts. |

700	ii.	Nathaniel Darling, born 12 January 1796 in Mendon, Massachusetts; died January 1798.
701	iii.	Cortez Darling, born 30 December 1797 in Mendon, Massachusetts; died 06 June 1798 in Mendon, Massachusetts.
702	iv.	George Darling, born 29 January 1800 in Mendon, Massachusetts; died June 1861. He married Ann Whetson 31 January 1821.
703	v.	Joanna Darling, born 10 July 1802 in Grafton, Massachusetts. She married Hiram Wilmarth 23 September 1829.
704	vi.	Nathaniel Darling, born 14 August 1804 in Grafton, Massachusetts; died 1866. He married Eleanor Burroughs 08 July 1830 in Mendon, Massachusetts.
705	vii.	Cortez Darling, born 19 October 1806 in Grafton, Massachusetts; died 1880. He married (1) Hannah Staples. He married (2) Prussia Saunders.
+ 706	viii.	Charles White Darling, born 24 December 1808 in Grafton, Massachusetts; died 03 March 1872.
707	ix.	Sarah Ann Darling, born 01 October 1813 in Smithfield, Rhode Island. She married Almon Thwing 13 September 1832.
708	x.	Benjamin Young Darling, born 09 July 1816 in Smithfield, Rhode Island. He married Rebecca Goggswell 05 April 1835.

333. Alpheus[5] Darling (Thomas[4], Benjamin[3], Denice[2], George[1]) was born 07 November 1773 in Mendon, Massachusetts. He married **Lois Kellogg** 22 December 1795. She was born 1777 in Mendon, Massachusetts.

Child of Alpheus Darling and Lois Kellogg is:
| 709 | i. | Alpheus[6] Darling, born 1798. |

Generation No. 5

346. Elizabeth[6] Hunt (Elizabeth[5] Darling, John[4], Captain John[3], Denice[2], George[1]) was born 09 June 1744 in Mendon, Massachusetts, and died 1790. She married **(1) Henry Aldrich** 24 November 1768 in Mendon, Massachusetts. She married **(2) Thomas Salisbury** 03 August 1778 in Norton Sub Hamdon,

Somerset, England, son of Samuel Salisbury and Mary Mitchell. He was born 1731 in Norton Sub Hamdon, Somerset, England, and died March 1816 in Norton-Sub-Hamdon, Somerset England.

More About Elizabeth Hunt:
Elizabeth Hunt Salisbury was buried on 19 April 1790, Norton-Sub-Hamdon, Somerset England

More About Thomas Salisbury:
Thomas Salisbury was baptized on 20 April 1735, Norton Sub Hamdon, Somerset, England.And he was buried on 22 March 1816, Norton-Sub-Hamdon, Somerset England

Children of Elizabeth Hunt and Thomas Salisbury are:
   710   i.   Martha[7] Salisbury, born 1778.

          More About Martha Salisbury:
          Martha Salisbury was baptized on 27 December 1778, Norton Sub Hamdon, Somerset, England

   711   ii.   Daniel Salisbury, born 17 May 1788 in Norton Sub Hamdon, Somerset, England; died 1809.

          More About Daniel Salisbury:
          Daniel Salisbury was baptized on 15 June 1788, Norton Sub Hamdon, Somerset, England, and he was buried on 09 March 1809, Norton-Sub-Hamdon, Somerset England

347. John[6] Darling (John[5], John[4], Captain John[3], Denice[2], George[1]) was born 24 April 1741 in Wrentham, Massachusetts, and died 1820 in Cumberland, Rhode Island. He married **Martha Barney** 15 May 1766 in Wrentham, Massachusetts, daughter of Thomas Barney and Martha Bruce.

Children of John Darling and Martha Barney are:
   712   i.   Pamelia[7] Darling, born 05 October 1766 in Cumberland, Rhode Island.
   713   ii.   Martha Darling, born 14 September 1768 in Cumberland, Rhode Island.

714	iii.	John Darling, born 02 August 1770 in Cumberland, Rhode Island.
715	iv.	Lorainia Darling, born 02 January 1771 in Cumberland, Rhode Island.
716	v.	James Darling, born 20 August 1773 in Cumberland, Rhode Island.
717	vi.	Gideon Darling, born 05 November 1777 in Cumberland, Rhode Island.
718	vii.	Joshua Darling, born 05 March 1781 in Cumberland, Rhode Island.
719	viii.	Jacob Darling, born 14 February 1785 in Cumberland, Rhode Island.

349. Hannah[6] Darling (John[5], John[4], Captain John[3], Denice[2], George[1]) was born 17 November 1744 in Wrentham, Massachusetts, and died 28 November 1819. She married **Timothy Bennett** 26 May 1765 in Cumberland, Rhode Island, son of John Bennett and Deborah Reynolds. He was born 1741 in Cumberland, Rhode Island, and died 19 October 1805 in Cumberland, Rhode Island.

Children of Hannah Darling and Timothy Bennett are:

720	i.	Levinah[7] Bennett, born 27 August 1765 in Cumberland, Rhode Island.
721	ii.	Joseph Bennett, born 06 November 1767 in Cumberland, Rhode Island.
722	iii.	Olive Bennett, born 16 February 1770 in Smithfield, Rhode Island.
723	iv.	Susanna Bennett, born 12 October 1772 in Cumberland, Rhode Island.
724	v.	Hannah Bennett, born 12 October 1774.
725	vi.	Timothy Bennett, born 12 June 1777 in Cumberland, Rhode Island.
726	vii.	Deborah Bennett, born 16 November 1781 in Cumberland, Rhode Island.

354. Rev. David[6] Darling (John[5], John[4], Captain John[3], Denice[2], George[1]) was born 14 April 1753 in Wrentham, Massachusetts, and died 15 March 1835 in New Hampshire. He married **(1) Esther Metcalf** 15 February 1781 in Wrentham,

Massachusetts, daughter of John Metcalf and Abigail Fisher. She was born 28 November 1761 in Wrentham, Massachusetts, and died 16 February 1793 in Keene, New Hampshire. He married **(2) Molly Woods** 24 September 1793 in Keene, New Hampshire. She was born 03 November 1766 in Keene, New Hampshire, and died 24 March 1817. He married **(3) Matilda Bowditch** 27 August 1818 in New Hampshire.

Children of Rev. Darling and Esther Metcalf are:

727	i.	John Metcalf[7] Darling, born 08 November 1782.
728	ii.	Nancy Darling, born 04 October 1786.
729	iii.	Fanny Darling, born 18 December 1788.
730	iv.	David Darling, born 19 July 1791.

Children of Rev. Darling and Molly Woods are:

731	i.	Molly[7] Darling, born 10 September 1794 in Keene, New Hampshire; died 10 September 1794 in Keene, New Hampshire.
732	ii.	Lydia Darling, born 10 September 1794 in Keene, New Hampshire; died 10 September 1794 in Keene, New Hampshire.
733	iii.	Elijiah Darling, born 28 December 1795.
734	iv.	Mary/Polly Darling, born 24 December 1796.
735	v.	Calvin Darling, born 18 July 1798.
736	vi.	Calvin Darling, born 10 February 1800 in Keene, New Hampshire; died 18 May 1875 in Iowa. He married Emily Steele.
737	vii.	Esther Darling, born 14 July 1801.
738	viii.	William Darling, born 11 November 1803.
739	ix.	James Darling, born 15 June 1805.
740	x.	Daniel Darling, born 15 May 1807 in Keene, New Hampshire; died 29 October 1890. He married (1) Betsey Whitemere. He married (2) Theodocia Stone.
741	xi.	Harriet Darling, born 01 August 1809.

358. Elias[6] Darling (John[5], John[4], Captain John[3], Denice[2], George[1]) was born 03 December 1759 in Wrentham, Massachusetts. He married **Nancy Alexander** 31 December 1789 in Cumberland, Rhode Island. She was born 1763 in Cumberland, Rhode Island.

Child of Elias Darling and Nancy Alexander is:
+ 742   i.   Nancy[7] Darling, born 12 August 1792 in Wrentham, Massachusetts.

360. Abel[6] Darling (John[5], John[4], Captain John[3], Denice[2], George[1]) was born 05 October 1766 in Wrentham, Massachusetts, and died 30 December 1826 in Medway, Massachusetts. He married **Mary/Polly Cobb** 17 February 1791 in Wrentham, Massachusetts, daughter of John Cobb and Huldah. She was born 10 June 1763 in Wrentham, Massachusetts.

Children of Abel Darling and Mary/Polly Cobb are:
    743   i.   Lois[7] Darling, born 03 July 1791 in Cumberland, Rhode Island.
+ 744   ii.   Samuel Darling, born 12 February 1793 in Cumberland, Rhode Island; died 02 October 1878 in Cumberland, Rhode Island.
    745   iii.   Mary Darling, born 05 February 1800 in Medway, Massachusetts.
+ 746   iv.   Nathan Darling, born 22 April 1802 in Medway, Massachusetts; died 16 July 1869.

367. Pelatiah[6] Darling (Pelatiah[5], John[4], Captain John[3], Denice[2], George[1]) was born 02 April 1760 in Mendon, Massachusetts, and died 03 April 1839 in Mendon, Massachusetts. He married **Phila Taft** 22 July 1790 in Mendon, Massachusetts. She was born 04 January 1772 in Mendon, Massachusetts, and died 02 September 1841 in Mendon, Massachusetts.

Notes for Pelatiah Darling
Pelatiah Darling and Phila Taft are both buried at the Chestnut Hill Meeting House Cemetery, located on Chestnut Hill Road in Millville, Massachusetts

Children of Pelatiah Darling and Phila Taft are:
+ 747   i.   Newton[7] Darling, born 22 August 1791 in Uxbridge, Massachusetts.

748	ii.	Maria Darling, born 22 March 1794 in Uxbridge, Massachusetts.
749	iii.	Newbury Darling, born 18 September 1797 in Uxbridge, Massachusetts.
750	iv.	Phila Darling, born 04 September 1800 in Uxbridge, Massachusetts.
+ 751	v.	Hannah Darling, born 07 May 1811 in Mendon, Massachusetts.

368. Joshua[6] Darling (Pelatiah[5], John[4], Captain John[3], Denice[2], George[1]) was born 19 August 1762 in Mendon, Massachusetts, and died 21 April 1834 in Uxbridge, Massachusetts. He married **(1) Patience**. He married **(2) Tabithia Handy** 06 March 1786 in Mendon, Massachusetts. She was born 1766 in Mendon, Massachusetts.

Children of Joshua Darling and Patience are:

+ 752	i.	Rufus[7] Darling, born 28 October 1807 in Mendon, Massachusetts.
753	ii.	Rozellany Darling, born 12 October 1809 in Mendon, Massachusetts.
754	iii.	Joshua Barney Darling, born 13 September 1815 in Mendon, Massachusetts.

Children of Joshua Darling and Tabithia Handy are:

755	i.	Helam[7] Darling, born 30 September 1786 in Uxbridge, Massachusetts.
756	ii.	Polly Darling, born 17 June 1788 in Uxbridge, Massachusetts.
757	iii.	Levory Darling, born 12 May 1790 in Uxbridge, Massachusetts.
758	iv.	Lyddia Darling, born 02 September 1793 in Uxbridge, Massachusetts.
759	v.	Lewis Darling, born 02 November 1794 in Uxbridge, Massachusetts.
760	vi.	Labiron Darling, born 04 November 1796 in Uxbridge, Massachusetts; died 03 July 1799 in Uxbridge, Massachusetts.
761	vii.	Daniel Franklin Darling, born 18 January 1799 in Uxbridge, Massachusetts.
762	viii.	Calvin Darling, born 16 July 1801 in Uxbridge, Massachusetts.

| 763 | ix. | Allister Darling, born 29 September 1803 in Uxbridge, Massachusetts. |
| 764 | x. | Margus Darling, born 20 November 1806 in Uxbridge, Massachusetts. |

371. Phineas[6] Darling (Pelatiah[5], John[4], Captain John[3], Denice[2], George[1]) was born 20 March 1769 in Mendon, Massachusetts, and died 1818 in Burrillville, Rhode Island. He married **(1) Bethia Kimton**. He married **(2) Mary Esten** 15 May 1802 in Mendon, Massachusetts, daughter of Joseph Esten and Sarah Prior. She was born in Glocester, Rhode Island.

Child of Phineas Darling and Bethia Kimton is:
| 765 | i. | John Kimton[7] Darling, born 1797 in Mendon, Massachusetts. |

Children of Phineas Darling and Mary Esten are:
	766	i.	Otis[7] Darling, born 02 February 1803 in Mendon, Massachusetts.
+	767	ii.	John Darling, born 13 June 1804 in Mendon, Massachusetts; died 05 June 1893 in Burrillville, Rhode Island.
	768	iii.	Phineas Darling, born 15 December 1805 in Mendon, Massachusetts.

376. Joseph[6] Albee (Ruth[5] Darling John[4], Captain John[3], Denice[2], George[1]) was born 1751, and died 07 May 1819 in Oxford, Massachusetts. He married **Mary Wheelock**. She was born 29 September 1746 in Uxbridge, Massachusetts.

Children of Joseph Albee and Mary Wheelock are:
769	i.	Emma[7] Albee, born 1771.
770	ii.	Obadiah Albee.
771	iii.	Daniel Albee.
772	iv.	Polly Albee.
773	v.	Prudence Albee.
774	vi.	Zerviah Albee.
775	vii.	Alpheus Albee, born 1784.
776	viii.	Joseph Albee.

777   ix.   John Albee.

379. Reuben[6] **Taft** (Elizabeth[5] Thayer, Ruth[4] Darling, Captain John[3], Denice[2], George[1]) was born 21 October 1742 in Uxbridge, Massachusetts. He married **(1) Thankful Thayer** 19 July 1761 in Uxbridge, Massachusetts. She was born 18 June 1744 in Mendon, Massachusetts. He married **(2) Faithful Thayer** 19 July 1761 in Uxbridge, Massachusetts, daughter of David Thayer and Jean Keith. She was born 18 June 1744 in Mendon, Massachusetts, and died 29 May 1831.

Child of Reuben Taft and Faithful Thayer is:
778   i.   Polly[7] Taft born 09 June 1773 in Uxbridge, Massachusetts; died 26 October 1848. She married Jesse Hurlbut.

383. Bathsheba[6] **Darling** (Joseph[5], Ebenezer[4], Captain John[3], Denice[2], George[1]) was born 30 January 1752 in Cumberland, Rhode Island. She married **Stephen Inman** 30 April 1769 in Cumberland, Rhode Island, son of Stephen Inman and Mary Barton. He was born 19 April 1750 in Cumberland, Rhode Island.

Children of Bathsheba Darling and Stephen Inman are:
779   i.   Rhoda[7] Inman.
780   ii.   Huldah Inman.

392. Simeon[6] **Darling** (Timothy[5], Ebenezer[4], Captain John[3], Denice[2], George[1]) was born 06 December 1769 in Bellingham, Massachusetts. He married **Peggy Vorce** 02 September 1793 in Bellingham, Massachusetts.

Children of Simeon Darling and Peggy Vorce are:
781   i.   Ruth[7] Darling, died 08 August 1800 in Bellingham, Massachusetts.
782   ii.   Simon Darling, born 1799; died 10 March 1801 in Bellingham, Massachusetts.

393. Abner⁶ Taft (Priscilla⁵ Thayer, Ruth⁴ Darling, Captain John³, Denice², George¹) was born 28 December 1736 in Uxbridge, Massachusetts, and died 30 May 1809. He married **Trial White** 25 November 1756 in Uxbridge, Massachusetts.. She was born 1737, and died 14 June 1814.

More About Abner Taft:
Abner Taft served in the Revolutionary War

Children of Abner Taft and Trial White are:
783	i.	Oliver⁷ Taft, born 01 May 1758 in Uxbridge, Massachusett; died 16 July 1775.
784	ii.	Webb Taft, born 26 March 1772.
785	iii.	Trial Taft, born 03 April 1777.
786	iv.	Darius Taft born 29 September 1763.
787	v.	Mary Taft, born 12 October 1767.
788	vi.	Moses Taft, born 29 September 1760; died 04 December 1848.

397. Nahum⁶ Taft (Priscilla⁵ Thayer, Ruth⁴ Darling, Captain John³, Denice², George¹) was born 17 August 1745 in Uxbridge, Massachusetts. He married **Rachel Albee** 19 February 1767.

Child of Nahum Taft and Rachel is:
+ 789	i.	Hannah⁷ Taft, died February 1839.

414. Reuben⁶ Thayer (Peter⁵, Ruth⁴ Darling, Captain John³, Denice², George¹) was born 27 June 1753, and died 09 June 1804 in New York. He married **Abigail White** 28 March 1777, daughter of Josiah White and Zipporah Wheelock. She was born 30 August 1759 in Uxbridge, Massachusetts, and died 22 June 1845.

Children of Reuben Thayer and Abigail White are:
790	i.	Chloe⁷ Thayer, born 08 November 1780. She married Archibald Clark
791	ii.	Abigail Thayer, born 11 October 1782; died 23 June 1841. She married Martin Lewis; born 1761.

792	iii.	Eunice Thayer, born 1785; died 1790.
793	iv.	Reuben Thayer, born 06 October 1786 in Uxbridge, Massachusetts; died 08 November 1860. He married Mary Vandevender.
794	v.	Sylvanus Thayer, born 1793
795	vi.	Eunice Thayer, born 05 March 1797.
796	vii.	George Washington Thayer, born 05 August 1799; died 07 March 1865 in New York. He married Martha P. Clemons August 1824; born 17 March 1804 in New York.

419. Peter⁶ Thayer (Peter⁵, Ruth⁴ Darling, Captain John³, Denice², George¹) was born 20 October 1755 in Mendon, Massachusetts. He married **Abigail Green** 01 October 1782 in Mendon, Massachusetts. She was born 1760 in Mendon, Massachusetts.

Children of Peter Thayer and Abigail Green are:

797	i.	Elizabeth⁷ Thayer, born 14 July 1784 in Mendon, Massachusetts.
798	ii.	Emery Thayer, born 27 January 1786 in Mendon, Massachusetts.
799	iii.	Samuel Thayer born 30 April 1788 in Mendon, Massachusetts.
+ 800	iv.	John H. Thayer, born 25 May 1791 in Mendon, Massachusetts.
+ 801	v.	Henry Thayer, born 23 March 1793 in Mendon, Massachusetts; died September 1849.
802	vi.	Peter Thayer, born 15 July 1795 in Mendon, Massachusetts.
803	vii.	Oliver Thayer, born 21 October 1796 in Mendon, Massachusetts.
804	viii.	Hyram Thayer, born 20 July 1800 in Mendon, Massachusetts.
805	ix.	Abigail Thayer, born 1803 in Mendon, Massachusetts.
806	x.	Sylvanus Thayer, born 09 August 1806 in Mendon, Massachusetts.

422. Joanna⁶ Darling (Samuel⁵, Samuel⁴, Captain John³, Denice², George¹) was born 10 October 1757 in Bellingham, Massachusetts, and died 06 February 1815. She married **Silas Cook** 07 November 1775 in Bellingham, Massachusetts, son of

Nathaniel Cook and Martha Ballou. He was born 23 March 1753 in Cumberland, Rhode Island, and died 12 February 1842.

Children of Joanna Darling and Silas Cook are:

807	i.	Reuben[7] Cook, born 27 December 1776 in Cumberland, Rhode Island.
808	ii.	Phila Cook, born 24 September 1778. She married Flavius Josephus Ballou.
809	iii.	Phebe Cook, born 16 July 1780. She married William Gaskill.
810	iv.	James Cook, born 27 May 1782. He married (1) Selina Cook. He married (2) Martha Moody.
811	v.	Silas Cook, born 23 February 1784.
812	vi.	Joanna Cook born 07 February 1786; died 15 February 1862 in Bellingham, Massachusetts. She married Stillman Rand 15 March 1830.
813	vii.	Olney Cook born 29 June 1788; died 24 January 1800 in Cumberland, Rhode Island.
+ 814	viii.	Ziba Cook, born 22 February 1791.
+ 815	ix.	Miranda Cook, born 09 April 1793; died 30 July 1887.
816	x.	Michael Cook, born 29 May 1796; died 29 September 1798 in Cumberland, Rhode Island.
817	xi.	Onley Cook, born 09 October 1801.
+ 818	xii.	Reuben Cook, born 27 December 1776 in Cumberland, Rhode Island; died 06 March 1867 in Bellingham, Massachusetts.
819	xiii.	Silas Cook, born 22 February 1784 in Cumberland, Rhode Island. He married Patience Sherman
820	xiv.	Michael Cook, born 23 November 1798.
821	xv.	Olney Cook, born 09 October 1801 in Cumberland, Rhode Island. He married Emily Draper.

423. Samuel[6] Darling (Samuel[5], Samuel[4], Captain John[3], Denice[2], George[1]) was born 08 August 1759 in Bellingham, Massachusetts, and died 16 January 1851. He married **Sarah Burr** 31 October 1782 in Bellingham, Massachusetts. She was born 14 June 1764 in Bellingham, Massachusetts, and died 31 January 1826 in Bellingham, Massachusetts.

Children of Samuel Darling and Sarah Burr are:

| + | 822 | i. | Asa[7] Darling, born 18 July 1783 in Bellingham, Massachusetts; died 16 July 1819 in Bellingham, Massachusetts. |
| | 823 | ii. | Collins Darling, born 14 October 1785 in Bellingham, Massachusetts; died 27 December 1843 in Bellingham, Massachusetts. |

Notes for Collins Darling:
Collins D arling is buried at the Center Cemetery, located on Rte 140 in Bellingham, Massachusetts

	824	iii.	Rhoda Darling, born 04 September 1787 in Bellingham, Massachusetts; died 17 October 1788 in Bellingham, Massachusetts.
+	825	iv.	Rhoda Darling, born 28 May 1789 in Bellingham, Massachusetts; died March 1854 in SUICIDE.
	826	v.	Esther Darling, born 08 July 1791 in Bellingham, Massachusetts. She married Stephen Sayles 11 January 1810 in Bellingham, Massachusetts.
+	827	vi.	Samuel Darling, born 14 August 1793 in Bellingham, Massachusetts; died 1874.
	828	vii.	Lanson Darling, born 09 October 1795 in Bellingham, Massachusetts; died 02 October 1796 in Bellingham, Massachusetts.
	829	viii.	Nancy Darling, born 23 December 1797 in Bellingham, Massachusetts. She married Elisha Capron 29 December 1818 in Bellingham, Massachusetts.
	830	ix.	Sarah Burr Darling, born 13 October 1800 in Bellingham, Massachusetts.
	831	x.	Caroline Darling, born 17 September 1801 in Bellingham, Massachusetts.
+	832	xi.	Jefferson Burr Darling, born 02 May 1803 in Bellingham, Massachusetts; died 10 July 1882 in Bellingham, Massachusetts.
	833	xii.	Caroline Darling, born 27 September 1806 in Bellingham, Massachusetts; died 29 September 1866 in Bellingham, Massachusetts.

427. Ziba[6] Darling (Samuel[5], Samuel[4], Captain John[3], Denice[2], George[1]) was born 19 September 1767 in Bellingham, Massachusetts, and died 29 October 1825 in Providence, Rhode Island. He married **(1) Vienna Ballou** 22 June 1796 in Bellingham, Massachusetts, daughter of Levi Ballou and Comfort

Thompson. She was born 29 January 1771 in Wrentham, Massachusetts, and died 09 January 1807. He married (2) **Freelove Thomas** 1808.

Children of Ziba Darling and Vienna Ballou are:

834   i.   Rhoda[7] Darling, born 1797 in Providence, Rhode Island; died 1872. She married Thaddeus Curtis 29 October 1827.

835   ii.   Welcome Ballou Darling, born 12 November 1798 in Providence, Rhode Island; died 06 April 1847. He married Seriah L. Olney

836   iii.   Vienna Darling, born 1800 in Providence, Rhode Island; died 25 September 1826. She married Thaddeus Curtis 01 June 1818.

837   iv.   Sarah Freeman Darling, born 1804 in Providence, Rhode Island. She married (1) Leonidas Whipple She married (2) Thomas Goff.

838   v.   Emily Darling, born 1807 in Providence, Rhode Island; died 06 June 1881.

+ 839   vi.   John Adams Darling, born 15 May 1802 in Providence, Rhode Island; died 14 July 1879 in Providence, Rhode Island.

431. Rhoda[6] Darling (Samuel[5], Samuel[4], Captain John[3], Denice[2], George[1]) was born 24 September 1776 in Bellingham, Massachusetts, and died 08 August 1843 in Bellingham, Massachusetts. She married (2) **Colonel Levi Cook** 05 October 1791, son of Deacon Cook and Dorcas Whipple. He was born 13 January 1773 in Cumberland, Rhode Island, and died 1857 in Cumberland, Rhode Island.

Children of Rhoda Darling and Colonel Cook are:

840   i.   Perley[7] Cook, born 05 August 1798. She married Olney Mason 28 December 1817.

841   ii.   Alpha Cook, born 24 April 1800.

842   iii.   Sally Cook, born 23 October 1801.

+ 843   iv.   Willis Cook, born 05 September 1803 in Cumberland, Rhode Island; died 11 February 1882.

+ 844   v.   Lyman Arnold Cook, born 17 March 1805 in Cumberland, Rhode Island; died 04 December 1898.

845   vi.   James Madison Cook, born 16 February 1809.

432. Olive[6] Darling (Samuel[5], Samuel[4], Captain John[3], Denice[2], George[1]) was born 30 June 1779 in Bellingham, Massachusetts, and died 1848. She married **Captain Amos Cook,** 15 August 1799, son of Deacon Cook and Dorcas Whipple. He was born 10 October 1776 in Cumberland, Rhode Island, and died 31 May 1853.

More About Olive Darling:
Olive Darling and her husband Captain Amos Cook are buried at the Rhode Island Historical Cemetery # 2, Cumberland Hill Road, in Woonsocket, Rhode Island.

Children of Olive Darling and Captain Cook are:

846   i. Ellis[7] Cook, born 26 August 1800 in Cumberland, Rhode Island; died 27 November 1880. He married Linda Follett 02 July 1820; died 10 March 1886.

More About Ellis Cook:
Ellis Cook is buried at the Rhode Island Historical Cemetery # 2, Cumberland Hill Road, Woonsocket, Rhode Island

More About Linda Follett:
Linda Follett is buried at the Rhode Island Historical Cemetery # 2, Cumberland Hill Road, Woonsocket, Rhode Island

847   ii. Arnold Cook, born 25 July 1802 in Cumberland, Rhode Island. He married Ella Ann Jillson 13 April 1826.

848   iii. Amos Cook, born 15 June 1804 in Cumberland, Rhode Island. He married Polly Follett 30 March 1823

849   iv. Davis Cook, born 27 May 1806 in Cumberland, Rhode Island; died 29 September 1840.

More About Davis Cook:
Davis Cook is buried at the Rhode Island Historical Cemetery # 2, Cumberland Hill Road, Woonsocket, Rhode Island

850   v. Eliza Cook, born 24 March 1808 in Cumberland, Rhode Island. She married (1) Otis D. Ballou. She married (2) A. Allen.

851	vi.	Barton Cook, born 05 September 1810 in Cumberland, Rhode Island; died 18 July 1849 in Uxbridge, Massachusetts. He married Lucy C. Wilkinsson, 03 October 1833.
852	vii.	Sally Cook, born 12 January 1813 in Cumberland, Rhode Island. She married Nathaniel Short 26 October 1832.
853	viii.	Olive Cook, born 01 January 1815 in Cumberland, Rhode Island. She married Samuel Lincoln 01 November 1838.
854	ix.	Olney M. Cook, born 01 January 1815 in Cumberland, Rhode Island; died 05 January 1876. He married Harriet Arnold 06 July 1836; born 18 January 1818; died 13 February 1896.

More About Olney M. Cook:
Olney M. Cook is buried at the Rhode Island Historical Cemetery # 2, Cumberland Hill Road, Woonsocket, Rhode Island

More About Harriet Arnold:
Harriet Arnold is buried at the Rhode Island Historical Cemetery # 2, Cumberland Hill Road, Woonsocket, Rhode Island

| 855 | x. | Levi Lee Cook, born 18 July 1817 in Cumberland, Rhode Island; died 26 February 1899. |

More About Levi Lee Cook:
Levi Lee Cook is buried at the Rhode Island Historical Cemetery # 2, Cumberland Hill Road, Woonsocket, Rhode Island

| 856 | xi. | Edmund L. Cook born 03 August 1820 in Cumberland, Rhode Island. He married Ann Eliza Mason 29 February 1844. |
| 857 | xii. | Albertus Cook, born 09 June 1823 in Cumberland, Rhode Island. He married Ann Haven 14 November 1846. |

445. Sarah[6] Draper (Jonathan[5], Mary[4] Darling, Captain John[3], Denice[2], George[1]) was born 1754. She married **James Prentice**

+ 858   i. Nahum[7] Prentice, born 08 May 1783 in Sutton,
            Massachusetts.

450. Molly[6] Draper (Jonathan[5], Mary[4] Darling, Captain John[3], Denice[2], George[1]) was born 1766. She married **Eddy Clark**.

Child of Molly Draper and Eddy Clark is:
+   859   i. Rachel[7] Clark, born 03 August 1792; died 09 March 1865.

464. Ahimaaz[6] Darling (Joshua[5], Samuel[4], Captain John[3], Denice[2], George[1]) was born 19 March 1765 in Bellingham, Massachusetts, and died 30 October 1836 in Bellingham, Massachusetts. He married **Mary Ballou/Wilcox** 07 September 1800 in Bellingham, Massachusetts. She was born 1774, and died 17 July 1849 in Bellingham, Massachusetts.

Notes for Ahimaaz Darling:
Ahimaaz Darling and his wife Mary are both buried at the Rakeville Cemetery, located on Lake Street in Bellingham, Massachusetts

Child of Ahimaaz Darling and Mary Ballou/Wilcox is:
+   860   i. Ahimaz[7] Darling, died 05 September 1874 in Bellingham, Massachusetts.

471. Benjamin[6] Wilson (Penelope[5] Darling, Samuel[4], Captain John[3], Denice[2], George[1]) He married **Phebe Merritt**.

Child of Benjamin Wilson and Phebe Merritt is:
+   861   i. Eliza[7] Wilson, born 09 April 1808; died 29 November 1853 in Willet, New York.

478. Alden[6] Darling (Timothy[5], David[4], Cornelius[3], Denice[2], George[1]) was born 1774, and died 1844 in New York. He married **Hannah Church** 1800. She was born 06 April 1780.

Children of Alden Darling and Hannah Church are:

862	i.	Richard[7] Darling, born 16 August 1803.
863	ii.	Timothy Darling, born 16 October 1804.
864	iii.	Alden Darling, born 25 December 1805.
865	iv.	John Darling, born 22 February 1813.
866	v.	Elizabeth Darling, born 15 January 1818.
867	vi.	Enoch Darling, born 1822.

481. Phebe[6] Darling (Cornelius[5], Cornelius[4], Cornelius[3], Denice[2], George[1]) was born 18 March 1767 in Bellingham, Massachusetts, and died 12 November 1861 in Bellingham, Massachusetts. She married **Jeremiah Crooks** 09 December 1787 in Bellingham, Massachusetts. He was born 16 December 1766 in Bellingham, Massachusetts, and died 17 February 1833 in Mendon, Massachusetts.

Children of Phebe Darling and Jeremiah Crooks are:

868	i.	Polly[7] Crooks, born 18 November 1788 in Bellingham, Massachusetts.
869	ii.	Jeremiah Crooks, born 10 June 1791 in Bellingham, Massachusetts.
870	iii.	Phebe Crooks, born 30 January 1796 in Bellingham, Massachusetts.
871	iv.	Sally Crooks, born 25 October 1798 in Bellingham, Massachusetts.
872	v.	Deborah Crooks, born 16 May 1801.
873	vi.	Joel Crooks, born 21 February 1803.

483. Asenath[6] Colman (Susannah[5] Martin, John[4], Hannah[3] Darling, Denice[2], George[1]) was born 07 October 1776, and died 04 December 1848. She married **Benjamin Allen** 04 February 1798, son of Phinehas Allen and Sarah Danforth. He was born 04 November 1777 in Lexington, Massachusetts, and died 19 October 1866 in Ashby, Massachusetts.

More About Benjamin Allen:
Benjamin Allen was a Farmer & shoemaker

Children of Asenath Colman and Benjamin Allen are:

+	874	i.	Henry[7] Allen, born 15 May 1798 in Ashby, Massachusetts; died 13 February 1885 in East Wallingfard, Vermont.
	875	ii.	Sarah Allen, born 07 August 1800 in Ashby, Massachusetts, died 22 August 1800 in Ashby, Massachusetts.
+	876	iii.	Louisa Allen, born 24 September 1801 in Ashby, Massachusetts; died 31 January 1874 in Newton, Massachusetts.
	877	iv.	Benjamin Allen, born 11 August 1803 in Ashby, Massachusetts; died 20 March 1831 in Amherst, Massachusetts...where he was in the graduating class
	878	v.	Zenas Allen, born 04 November 1805 in Ashby, Massachusetts; died 20 May 1887 in Hyde Park. He married (1) Caroline Randall 11 September 1827; born 05 March 1805 in Ashburnham, Massachusetts; died 13 March 1869 in Hyde Park. He married (2) Charlotte Maynard (Clarke) Sanders 23 March 1870 in New Ipswich, New Hampshire; born 18 February 1822 in Whateley, Massachusetts.
	879	vi.	Sidney Allen, born 15 June 1808 in Ashburnham, Massachusetts; died 19 June 1877 in Newton, Massachusetts. He married (1) Harriet Lewis 14 August 1834; died 31 July 1846 in Boston, Massachusetts He married (2) Emeline Darling Walcott 10 January 1847; died 17 February 1881 in Newton, Massachusetts.
	880	vii.	Samuel Martin Allen, born 12 May 1813 in Ashby, Massachusetts. He married Nancy Smith Kendall 26 April 1840; born 19 May 1816; died 11 December 1895 in Ashby, Massachusetts.
	881	viii.	Charles Stimson Allen, born 03 January 1820 in Ashby, Massachusetts He married (1) Lucy Ann Hubbard 16 August 1842; born 04 March 1824; died 17 November 1860 in Ashby, Massachusetts. He married (2) Sarah Caroline Hubbard 27 June 1860; born 19 June 1837 in Ashby, Massachusetts.

485. Jarvis[6] Thayer (Silas[5], Abigail[4] Darling, Daniel[3], Denice[2], George[1]) was born 20 November 1770 in Mendon, Massachusetts, and died January 1834. He married **Susan Parker** 1796. She died 1832.

Children of Jarvis Thayer and Susan Parker are:

882	i.	Nahum Pond[7] Thayer, born 31 July 1802; died October 1851 in Michigan. He married Lavina.

883	ii.	John B. Thayer, born 10 November 1798.
884	iii.	Jarvis Thayer, born 1802
885	iv.	Simeon Thayer.
886	v.	Cyrus Thayer
887	vi.	Almira Thayer.
888	vii.	Nancy Thayer, born 1813.
889	viii.	Perley Thayer, born 26 June 1815.
890	ix.	Elizabeth Thayer, born 24 May 1818.

498. William H.[6] Thayer (Silas[5], Abigail[4] Darling, Daniel[3], Denice[2], George[1]) was born 13 February 1801 in Mendon, Massachusetts, and died 22 August 1844 He married **(1) Olivia Thayer**. She died 1827. He married **(2) Mary Thayer** 21 February 1829. She was born 09 December 1802.

Child of William Thayer and Mary Thayer is:
891	i.	John H.[7] Thayer, born 15 September 1832 He married Mary Smith 21 October 1851.

517. Elisha[6] Darling (Job[5], Samuel[4], Daniel[3], Denice[2], George[1]) was born 1776, and died 10 July 1858 in Burrillville, Rhode Island. He married **Ruth Walling** 1795, daughter of Jacob Walling and Martha Phillips. She was born 1775.

Children of Elisha Darling and Ruth Walling are:
	892	i.	Jacob[7] Darling, born 1802 in Burrillville, Rhode Island.
	893	ii.	Martha Darling, born 1805 in Burrillville, Rhode Island.
+	894	iii.	Maria Darling, born 1808 in Burrillville, Rhode Island; died 08 December 1861 in Burrillville, Rhode Island.
	895	iv.	Isaac Darling, born 1811. He married Fidelia Belone; born 1816.
	896	v.	Ruth Darling, born 1814 in Burrillville, Rhode Island.
	897	vi.	George Darling, born 1817 in Burrillville, Rhode Island.

527. Lyman[6] Darling (Benson[5], Samuel[4], Daniel[3], Denice[2], George[1]) was born 08 February 1803 in Mendon, Massachusetts, and died 18 October 1873 in Mendon, Massachusetts. He married **Lucy Stearns** 14 April 1824 in Medfield, Massachusetts, daughter of Nathan Stearns and Mary Turner. She was born 1804, and died 25 September 1896 in Mendon, Massachusetts.

Children of Lyman Darling and Lucy Stearns are:

898   i.   Susan Stearns[7] Darling, born 20 February 1826; died 1905. She married (1) Francis Irons. She married (2) William Gassett. She married (3) Luther Guild.

899   ii.   George Seth Darling, born 20 January 1828 in Mendon, Massachusetts; died 19 November 1885 in Connecticut. He married Eliza S. Carter 03 July 1850 in East Greenwich, Rhode Island.

900   iii.   Lyman Augustus Darling, born 20 February 1830 in Mendon, Massachusetts; died 10 May 1901. He married Margaret Carter in East Greenwich, Rhode Island.

901   iv.   Harriet Darling, born 27 March 1832 in Mendon, Massachusetts; died 22 May 1832 in Mendon, Massachusetts.

902   v.   Charles Darling, born 23 January 1834 in Mendon, Massachusetts; died 26 August 1836 in Uxbridge, Massachusetts.

903   vi.   James Benson Darling, born 23 January 1834 in Mendon, Massachusetts; died 26 August 1836 in Uxbridge, Massachusetts.

904   vii.   Henry Darling, born 30 May 1836 in Mendon, Massachusetts. He married Lydia McGrafth 30 December 1857.

905   viii.   Nancy Ann Darling, born 25 August 1838 in Milford, Massachusetts. She married Levi L. Hanley 30 December 1857 in Uxbridge, Massachusetts.

906   ix.   Elizabeth R. Darling, born 11 November 1841 in Medfield, Massachusetts. She married Sidney Goodell.

+   907   x.   James Edmond Darling, born 1843 in Medfield, Massachusetts.

908   xi.   Caroline Idelia Darling, born 12 February 1846 in Medfield, Massachusetts. She married Henry Renuck 13 June 1866 in Mendon, Massachusetts.

909   xii.   Harriet Darling, born 29 June 1848 in Medfield, Massachusetts; died 01 March 1861 in Mendon, Massachusetts.

528. Artemus[6] Darling (Benson[5], Samuel[4], Daniel[3], Denice[2], George[1]) was born 07 April 1798 in Mendon, Massachusetts, and died 19 April 1861 in Providence, Rhode Island. He married

Lorinda Taft 05 November 1826 in Mendon, Massachusetts. She was born 14 February 1802 in Mendon, Massachusetts.

Notes for Artemus Darling:
Artemus Darling and his wife Lorinda Taft are buried at the Swan Point Cemetery, located on Blackstone Blvd. in Providence, Rhode Island

Children of Artemus Darling and Lorinda Taft are:

910   i.   Idelia Taft[7] Darling, born 14 October 1828 in Mendon, Massachusetts; died 10 September 1829 in Mendon, Massachusetts.

911   ii.   Caroline Idelia Darling, born 18 May 1830 in Mendon, Massachusetts; died 18 March 1831 in Mendon, Massachusetts.

912   iii.   Mary Sophia Darling, born 28 January 1833 in Mendon, Massachusetts; died 11 August 1910 in Providence, Rhode Island. She married Edward Arnold Luther 15 October 1855 in Providence, Rhode Island; born 1834.

Notes for Mary Sophia Darling:
Sophia Darling is buried at the Locust Grove Cemetery, located on Elmwood Avenue in Providence, Rhode Island

913   iv.   Nancy Jane Darling, born 22 April 1835 in Mendon, Massachusetts; died 11 August 1836 in Mendon, Massachusetts.

914   v.   Artemus Amasa Darling, born 27 May 1836 in Mendon, Massachusetts.

915   vi.   Seth Benson Darling, born 12 January 1838 in Mendon, Massachusetts; died 15 September 1868.

Notes for Seth Benson Darling:
Seth Benson Darling is also buried at the Swan Point Cemetery

916   vii.   Edward Everett Darling, born 30 October 1839 in Mendon, Massachusetts; died 02 May 1918 in Providence, Rhode Island.

+   917   viii.   Moses Oscar Darling, born 07 August 1841 in Mendon, Massachusetts; died 05 March 1891 in Johnston, Rhode Island.

531. Mary Susan⁶ Taft (Jemima⁵ Thompson, Susannah⁴ Darling, Daniel³, Denice², George¹) was born 1781 in Danby, Vermont, and died 1862. She married **Manasseh Sprague,** son of Joseph Sprague and Mary Thompson. He was born 1775 in Danby, Vermont, and died 26 March 1858 in Huntington, Vermont.

Children of Mary Taft and Manasseh Sprague are:

+ 918   i.   Joseph⁷ Sprague, born 29 April 1796 in Huntington, Vermont; died 19 December 1875.
+ 919   ii.   Gideon Sprague, born 1806 in Wallingford, Vermont; died 12 December 1884 in Huntington, Vermont.
   920   iii.   George Sprague.
+ 921   iv.   Phineas Sprague, born 1819 in Wallingford, Vermont; died ca 1895 in Huntingto, Vermont.
+ 922   v.   Manassah Sprague, died 07 February 1886 in Horicon, Warren County, New York.
   923   vi.   Jemima Sprague, born 28 January 1820. She married Nathaniel Cook.
   924   vii.   Mary Sprague, born 21 July 1821; died 28 March 1864. She married Josiah Strong 22 October 1844.

532. Mary Susan⁶ Taft (Jemima⁵ Thompson, Susannah⁴ Darling, Daniel³, Denice², George¹) was born 1781 in Danby, Vermont, and died 1862. She married **Manasseh Sprague**, son of Joseph Sprague and Mary Thompson. He was born 1775 in Danby, Vermont, and died 26 March 1858 in Huntington, Vermont.

534. Sarah⁶ Hunt (Peter⁵, Kezia⁴ Darling, Daniel³, Denice², George¹) died 28 January 1892. She married **Peter Church**, son of Joseph Church and Elizabeth Taylor. He was born 1799, and died 25 August 1866 in Middletown, Rhode Island.

More About Peter Church:
Peter Church was a Sergeant in the Rhode Island Militia...Dorr War

Children of Sarah Hunt and Peter Church are:

927   i.   Henry Augustus[7] Church, born 01 August 1831. He married Henrietta Winch 07 January 1886.

928   ii.   William Marshall Church, born 17 June 1833; died 09 January 1834.

929   iii.   Mary Elizabeth Church, born 20 December 1834. She married Cyrus Butler.

930   iv.   Sarah Church, born 20 March 1846. She married William H. Howell.

931   v.   George M. Church, born 29 November 1837

535. Cyrus[6] Darling (Zeleck[5], William[4], Daniel[3], Denice[2], George[1]) was born 01 September 1787 in Sutton, Massachusetts. He married **Sophia Thayer** 02 November 1811 in Sutton, Massachusetts.

Children of Cyrus Darling and Sophia Thayer are:

932   i.   Luann[7] Darling, born 24 November 1814 in Sutton, Massachusetts.

933   ii.   Estes Darling, born 10 November 1817 in Sutton, Massachusetts.

934   iii.   Adeline Darling, born 29 August 1822 in Sutton, Massachusetts.

536. Wheeler[6] Darling (Zeleck[5], William[4], Daniel[3], Denice[2], George[1]) was born 19 November 1789 in Sutton, Massachusetts. He married **Sybille Thayer** 13 October 1811 in Sutton, Massachusetts.

Child of Wheeler Darling and Sybille Thayer is:

935   i.   Charles Wheeler[7] Darling, born 14 August 1812 in Sutton, Massachusetts.

538. Zelek[6] Darling (Zeleck[5], William[4], Daniel[3], Denice[2], George[1]) was born 16 February 1794 in Sutton, Massachusetts. He married **Sarah Ann**.

Children of Zelek Darling and Sarah Ann are:

936	i.	Edwin Crawford[7] Darling, born 11 March 1818 in Providence, Rhode Island.
+ 937	ii.	Eleanor Darling, born 23 September 1820 in Providence, Rhode Island.
938	iii.	Rodney Luther Darling, born 06 November 1822 in Douglas, Massachusetts.
939	iv.	Melancy Lawton Darling, born 02 April 1830 in Sutton, Massachusetts.

580. Rowena[6] Wheelock (Paul[5], Deborah[4] Darling, Benjamin[3], Denice[2], George[1]) was born 20 December 1760 in of Uxbridge, Massachusetts, and died 1802. She married **Nicholas Salisbury** 15 March 1787 in Glocester, Rhode Island, son of Edward Salisbury and Abigail Hawkins. He was born 02 April 1762 in Glocester, Rhode Island, and died 10 December 1833.

More About Rowena Wheelock:
Rowena Wheelock Salisbury is buried at the Rural Cemetery, Adams, New York.

Notes for Nicholas Salisbury:
Nicholas Salisbury was one of the first settlers in Adams, New York. In the spring of 1800, he started out for his new home. He arrived on 26 April 1800. Nicholas Salisbury was an active and successful settler and, afterwards, attained a position of prominence in the town. He was the first supervisor and held office until 1814.

More About Nicholas Salisbury:
Nicholas Salisbury is buried at the Rural Cemetery, Adams, New York.

Children of Rowena Wheelock and Nicholas Salisbury are:

+   940   i.   Sarah[7] Salisbury.
     941   ii.   Edward Salisbury
     942   iii.   Lucy Salisbury. She married Dr. Walter Webb; born 04 October 1794 in Hoosiuk Falls, New York.
+   943   iv.   Lydia Salisbury, born 03 September 1788; died 11 August 1837.
     944   v.   Silas Salisbury, born 1789; died 1873   He married Nancy Cubock-Harris; born 1802; died 1870.
     945   vi.   Abigail Salisbury, born 15 February 1790; died 27 May 1875. She married Benjamin Rudd 30 September 1830.
+   946   vii.   Seneca Sales Salisbury, born 1794; died 1889 in Clayton, Kansas.

582. Jerusha[6] Darling (Joseph[5], Joseph[4], Benjamin[3], Denice[2], George[1]) was born 15 March 1761 in Mendon, Massachusetts. She married **Peter Darling** 01 January 1778 in Cumberland, Rhode Island, son of Peter Darling and Priscilla Cook. He was born 22 August 1757 in Cumberland, Rhode Island, and died 13 November 1796 in Cumberland, Rhode Island.

Children are listed above under (280) Peter Darling

602. Thomas Jefferson[6] Darling (Jacob[5], Joseph[4], Benjamin[3], Denice[2], George[1]) was born 1784 in Hebron, New York, and died 1865 in Indiana. He married **Ruth Ann Beach** 1804 in New York. She was born 02 October 1785 in Connecticut, and died 13 April 1866.

Children of Thomas Darling and Ruth Beach are:

     947   i.   Thomas Jefferson[7] Darling, born 20 November 1807 in New York; died 12 January 1881. He married Julianne Martin 31 March 1827 in Indiana; born 18 June 1810 in Kentucky.
+   948   ii.   Margery Darling, born 1807.
     949   iii.   Peter Darling, born 23 February 1809; died 19 May 1881 in Indiana.
     950   iv.   George Darling, born 1813 in New York. He married Maria Snell.

951	v.	David Darling, born 27 December 1818 in Indiana; died 21 July 1858 in Illinois.
952	vi.	Mary Jane Darling, born 1824. She married Manley Hunter 10 January 1839 in Indiana.
953	vii.	Ruth Darling, born 09 September 1825 in Indiana; died 06 January 1887 in Indiana.

604. James C.[6] Darling (Jacob[5], Joseph[4], Benjamin[3], Denice[2], George[1]) was born 1786 in New York. He married **Diana Ferris**, daughter of Lewis Ferris and Lovica. She was born 1783.

Children of James Darling and Diana Ferris are:

954	i.	Lydia[7] Darling.
955	ii.	Isaac Darling.
956	iii.	Elizabeth Darling.
957	iv.	Mary Ann Darling.
958	v.	Melissa Darling.
959	vi.	Phoebe Darling.
960	vii.	Sarah Darling.

611. David[6] Darling (David[5], Ebenezer[4], Benjamin[3], Denice[2], George[1]) was born 12 January 1768 in Glocester, Rhode Island, and died 25 October 1846 in North Adams, Massachusetts. He married **Abigail Hodge** 18 August 1786. She was born 1765 in Glocester, Rhode Island, and died 24 January 1813 in North Adams, Massachusetts.

Children of David Darling and Abigail Hodge are:

961	i.	George[7] Darling, born 30 March 1787.
962	ii.	Oliver Darling, born 12 February 1789 in Glocester, Rhode Island; died 12 January 1842.
963	iii.	Andrew Darling, born 15 May 1791 in Glocester, Rhode Island; died 13 July 1802.
964	iv.	David Allen Darling, born 14 February 1793 in Glocester, Rhode Island; died 09 August 1853.
965	v.	Polly Darling, born 04 November 1794 in Glocester, Rhode Island.
966	vi.	Sarah Darling, born 23 March 1796 in Glocester, Rhode Island.

967	vii.	William Darling, born 31 December 1798 in Glocester, Rhode Island; died 11 March 1802 in Glocester, Rhode Island.
968	viii.	Nabby Darling, born 19 June 1800 in Glocester, Rhode Island; died 18 March 1802 in Glocester, Rhode Island.
969	ix.	William Darling, born 21 May 1805 in Glocester, Rhode Island; died 29 April 1836.
970	x.	Rebecca Darling, born 11 July 1807; died 17 October 1867. She married Preserved Eddy 1823; born 1799.
971	xi.	Henry Darling, born 22 September 1809 in Glocester, Rhode Island.

620. Andrew⁶ Darling (Andrew⁵, Ebenezer⁴, Benjamin³, Denice², George¹) was born 1790 in Burrillville, Rhode Island. He married **Phebe Burdish**.

Child of Andrew Darling and Phebe Burdish is:

972	i.	Horace⁷ Darling, born 1816 in Burrillville, Rhode Island; died 1901.

622. Darius⁶ Darling (Ebenezer⁵, Ebenezer⁴, Benjamin³, Denice², George¹) was born 1781 in Glocester, Rhode Island, and died 14 December 1861 in Glocester, Rhode Island. He married **Susannah Herendeen**, daughter of Reuben Bowen and Dorothy Whitmore. She was born 1787.

Children of Darius Darling and Susannah Herendeen are:

+	973	i.	Esseck⁷ Darling, born 1808 in Glocester, Rhode Island; died 24 July 1889 in Woodstock, Connecticut.
+	974	ii.	Nelson Darling, born October 1828 in Glocester, Rhode Island; died 20 December 1878 in Glocester, Rhode Island.
	975	iii.	George Darling, born 1830 in Glocester, Rhode Island; died 15 January 1901 in Cranston, Rhode Island.
	976	iv.	James Darling, born 1832 in Glocester, Rhode Island; died 01 January 1857 in Glocester, Rhode Island.

623. William⁶ Darling (Ebenezer⁵, Ebenezer⁴, Benjamin³, Denice², George¹) was born December 1777 in Glocester, Rhode Island, and died 01 July 1811 in Glocester, Rhode Island. He married **Betsey Wade**, daughter of William Wade and Mary Angell. She was born 1771 in Glocester, Rhode Island.

Children of William Darling and Betsey Wade are:
+ 977   i.   Angell[7] Darling, born 1797 in Glocester, Rhode Island.
+ 978   ii. Sarah Ann Darling, born 28 August 1798 in Glocester, Rhode Island; died 05 April 1885 in Glocester, Rhode Island.
   979   iii. Fidelia Darling, born 1807 in Glocester, Rhode Island; died 1897 in Glocester, Rhode Island. She married Mathewson Paine; born in Glocester, Rhode Island.
+ 980   iv. Riley Darling, born 09 September 1810 in Glocester, Rhode Island; died 25 January 1907 in East Greenwich, Rhode Island.

644. Welcome Greene[6] Darling (Welcome[5], Peter[4], Benjamin[3], Denice[2], George[1]) was born 29 October 1810 in Cumberland, Rhode Island, and died 26 April 1870 in Woonsocket, Rhode Island. He married **(1) Sarah Barney** 27 September 1832 in Cumberland, Rhode Island. She was born in Wrentham, Massachusetts. He married **(2) Marieta P. Jillson** 25 October 1837, daughter of Nathan Jillson and Susannah Taft. She was born 27 May 1815 in Cumberland, Rhode Island.

Child of Welcome Darling and Sarah Barney is:
   981   i.   James G.[7] Darling.

Children of Welcome Darling and Marieta Jillson are:
   982   i.   Anna Sarah[7] Darling, born 01 November 1838 in Woonsocket, Rhode Island.
   983   ii. Albert Darling, born 13 June 1841 in Woonsocket, Rhode Island.
   984   iii. Erwin Darling, born 07 February 1849 in Woonsocket, Rhode Island; died 07 March 1850 in Woonsocket, Rhode Island.
   985   iv. Alston Darling, born 27 April 1852 in Woonsocket, Rhode Island.
   986   v.   Edmond Darling, born 10 April 1854 in Woonsocket, Rhode Island.

987   vi.   Barton Darling, born 17 July 1858 in Woonsocket, Rhode Island.

673. Henry[6] Darling (Henry[5], Samuel[4], Benjamin[3], Denice[2], George[1]) was born 20 March 1784 in Smithfield, Rhode Island. He married **Mary Wilbur** 13 December 1805 in Smithfield, Rhode Island.

Children of Henry Darling and Mary Wilbur are:

+   988   i.   William Smith[7] Darling, born 02 June 1808 in Smithfield, Rhode Island.

989   ii.   Dennis Albert Darling, born 12 September 1810 in Smithfield, Rhode Island.

695. Thomas[6] Darling (Simeon[5], Thomas[4], Benjamin[3], Denice[2], George[1]) was born 21 June 1785 in Mendon, Massachusetts, and died 15 November 1870 in Indiana. He married **Theodocia Russell** 10 October 1808 in Massachusetts, daughter of Solomon Russell and Sarah Rice. She was born 19 November 1787 in Massachusetts, and died 10 November 1857 in Indiana.

Children of Thomas Darling and Theodocia Russell are:

990   i.   Rowena[7] Darling, born 22 November 1809; died 03 November 1850. She married Ansel Edwards.

991   ii.   Thomas West Darling, born 15 August 1811; died 03 January 1892.

992   iii.   Solomon Darling, born 22 December 1813.

993   iv.   Anna Darling, born 04 March 1815.

994   v.   Elizabeth Darling, born 20 December 1819.

995   vi.   Rufus Darling, born 28 April 1822.

996   vii.   Mary Darling, born 11 April 1824.

997   viii.   Levi Lincoln Darling, born 03 October 1825. He married Catherine Jones 12 April 1848 in New York; born 24 March 1824.

998   ix.   Isabella Darling, born 22 March 1829.

999   x.   Nelson Strong Darling, born 04 October 1821.

1000   xi.   Mary Ann Darling, born 1817.

706. Charles White^6 Darling (Nathan^5, Thomas^4, Benjamin^3, Denice^2, George^1) was born 24 December 1808 in Grafton, Massachusetts, and died 03 March 1872. He married **Lydia Cole** 02 February 1828 in Dedham, Massachusetts, daughter of James Cole and Lavinia Cook. She was born 21 October 1810, and died 30 March 1882 in Natick, Massachusetts.

Children of Charles Darling and Lydia Cole are:

1001	i.	George Barney^7 Darling, born 12 November 1827 in Northbridge, Massachusetts; died 03 March 1879.
1002	ii.	Charles Darling, born 02 February 1830; died 15 March 1911 in Natick, Massachusetts.
1003	iii.	Albert Darling, born 13 March 1832; died 17 August 1941 in Woonsocket, Rhode Island.
1004	iv.	Simon Darling, born 13 March 1832; died 15 August 1832.
1005	v.	Mary Young Darling, born 19 September 1834; died 01 June 1905. She married George Barney Lee 31 December 1850 in Medford, Massachusetts.
1006	vi.	Charles Darling, born 17 June 1837; died 15 March 1911 in Natick, Massachusetts. He married Katherine Thomas.
1007	vii.	William Darling, born 07 September 1840 in Woonsocket, Rhode Island; died 19 August 1848 in Woonsocket, Rhode Island.
1008	viii.	Albert Darling, born 09 March 1843 in Woonsocket, Rhode Island; died 15 March 1917 in Maine.
1009	ix.	Lydia Darling, born 10 December 1847 in Woonsocket, Rhode Island. She married James Richards.
1010	x.	James Darling, born 27 December 1850 in Woonsocket, Rhode Island; died 1922.

Generation No. 6

742. Nancy^7 Darling (Elias^6, John^5, John^4, Captain John^3, Denice^2, George^1) was born 12 August 1792 in Wrentham, Massachusetts. She married **Elias Blake** 01 January 1811 in Wrentham, Massachusetts. He was born 25 July 1792 in Wrentham, Massachusetts.

Children of Nancy Darling and Elias Blake are:

1011	i.	Nancy^8 Blake, born 10 September 1811 in Wrentham, Massachusetts.

1012	ii.	Elias Blake, born 12 February 1815 in Wrentham, Massachusetts.
1013	iii.	Samuel Blake, born 30 May 1817 in Wrentham, Massachusetts.
1014	iv.	Jeremiah Darling Blake, born 21 June 1820 in Wrentham, Massachusetts.

744. Samuel[7] Darling (Abel[6], John[5], John[4], Captain John[3], Denice[2], George[1]) was born 12 February 1793 in Cumberland, Rhode Island, and died 02 October 1878 in Cumberland, Rhode Island. He married **Sophia Dobbs** 1825. She was born 1803, and died 08 November 1889 in Medway, Massachusetts.

Children of Samuel Darling and Sophia Dobbs are:

1015	i.	Eli[8] Darling, born 1827.
1016	ii.	Jesse Darling, born 1828.
1017	iii.	Emma Jane Darling, born 1834.
1018	iv.	Eunice Darling, born 1837.
1019	v.	Lucinia Darling, born 15 November 1840.
1020	vi.	Samatha Darling, born 16 March 1842.
1021	vii.	Marshall Darling, born 1844.

746. Nathan[7] Darling (Abel[6], John[5], John[4], Captain John[3], Denice[2], George[1]) was born 22 April 1802 in Medway, Massachusetts, and died 16 July 1869. He married **(1) Anna Lovering** 17 May 1826. He married **(2) Harriet Leonard** 16 August 1843.

Children of Nathan Darling and Harriet Leonard are:

1022	i.	David Sanford[8] Darling, born 14 April 1844.
1023	ii.	Mary Darling, born 07 December 1845.
1024	iii.	Harriet Darling, born 15 October 1849.

747. Newton[7] Darling (Pelatiah[6], Pelatiah[5], John[4], Captain John[3], Denice[2], George[1]) was born 22 August 1791 in Uxbridge, Massachusetts. He married **Malyna**. She was born 1798, and died 07 May 1847 in Uxbridge, Massachusetts.

Child of Newton Darling and Malyna is:

1025   i.   Josephine[8] Darling, born 1829; died 26 December 1837 in
                Uxbridge, Massachusetts.

751. Hannah[7] Darling (Pelatiah[6], Pelatiah[5], John[4], Captain
John[3], Denice[2], George[1]) was born 07 May 1811 in Mendon,
Massachusetts. She married **Rufus Ballou** 22 December 1842 in
Milford, Massachusetts, son of Dennis Ballou and Mercy Taft. He
was born 17 November 1809 in Smithfield, Rhode Island.

Children of Hannah Darling and Rufus Ballou are:

1026   i.   Julia Ann[8] Ballou, born 01 November 1849 in Smithfield,
                Rhode Island.
1027   ii.   Rufus Willis Ballou, born 31 March 1855 in Smithfield,
                Rhode Island.

752. Rufus[7] Darling (Joshua[6], Pelatiah[5], John[4], Captain
John[3], Denice[2], George[1]) was born 28 October 1807 in Mendon,
Massachusetts. He married **Lucinda Alexander** 04 December
1834 in Mendon, Massachusetts.

Children of Rufus Darling and Lucinda Alexander are:

1028   i.   Charlotte Amanda[8] Darling, born 08 March 1836 in
                Mendon, Massachusetts.
1029   ii.   George Samuel Darling born 20 June 1847 in Mendon,
                Massachusetts.

767. John[7] Darling (Phineas[6], Pelatiah[5], John[4], Captain
John[3], Denice[2], George[1]) was born 13 June 1804 in Mendon,
Massachusetts, and died 05 June 1893 in Burrillville, Rhode
Island. He married **Susannah Harris** 24 November 1830 in
Burrillville, Rhode Island, daughter of George Harris and Nancy
Phillips. She was born 1814 in Mendon, Massachusetts, and died
17 December 1865 in Burrillville, Rhode Island.

Notes for John Darling

John Darling is buried at the Pascoag Cemetery, located in Burrillville, Rhode Island

Children of John Darling and Susannah Harris are:

	1030	i.	John Quincy[8] Darling, born 15 April 1834 in Burrillville, Rhode Island; died 1914. He married Mary Taft 1860 in Burrillville, Rhode Island.
	1031	ii.	Susan Alvina Darling, born 03 December 1835 in Burrillville, Rhode Island. She married Daniel Esten; died in Douglas, Massachusetts.
+	1032	iii.	George Darling, born 05 May 1840 in Burrillville, Rhode Island.
+	1033	iv.	William Darling, born 29 September 1844 in Burrillville, Rhode Island; died 21 August 1886 in Burrillville, Rhode Island.
	1034	v.	Amos Darling, born 13 September 1846 in Burrillville, Rhode Island. He married Ellen Jenks.
+	1035	vi.	Esek Darling, born 13 September 1842.

789. Hannah[7] Taft (Nahum[6], Priscilla[5] Thayer, Ruth[4] Darling, Captain John[3], Denice[2], George[16] died February 1839. She married **Artemus Thayer** 25 April 1788 in Mendon, Massachusetts, son of Pelatiah Thayer and Hannah Thayer. He was born 20 February 1765 in Mendon, Massachusetts, and died 15 February 1841.

Children of Hannah Taft and Artemus Thayer are:

+	1036	i.	Labin[8] Thayer, born 09 February 1793.
	1037	ii.	Rachel Thayer, born 02 February 1797.
+	1038	iii.	Pelatiah Thayer, born 03 January 1800 in Mendon, Massachusetts; died 07 October 1849 in Bellingham, Massachusetts.
	1039	iv.	Miranda Thayer, born 19 February 1804. She married Francis Cook 08 April 1820
	1040	v.	Hannah Thayer, born 12 April 1809. She married Elial Barber 14 September 1833
+	1041	vi.	Artemus Thayer, born 1813; died 1888.

800. John H.[7] Thayer (Peter[6], Peter[5], Ruth[4] Darling, Captain John[3], Denice[2], George[1]) was born 25 May 1791 in Mendon, Massachusetts .He married **Susan Mitchell Simmon** 15 February 1820 in Mendon, Massachusetts, daughter of John Simmon and Ruth Mitchell. She was born 06 June 1787 in Easton, Massachusetts.

Child of John Thayer and Susan Simmon is:
    1042   i.   Lucinda Ann[8] Thayer, born 02 November 1826 in Braintree, Massachusetts. She married Lewis Thayer 22 February 1849; born 1807.

801. Henry[7] Thayer (Peter[6], Peter[5], Ruth[4] Darling, Captain John[3], Denice[2], George[1]) was born 23 March 1793 in Mendon, Massachusetts, and died September 1849. He married (1) **Mary Moon** 1816, daughter of Abraham Moon and Mary Cooper. She was born 1797, and died 28 December 1826 in New York. He married (2) **Betsey Hall** 1830.

Children of Henry Thayer and Mary Moon are:
+   1043   i.   George Washington[8] Thayer, born 28 February 1817.
    1044   ii.   Robert Thayer, born 27 February 1819. He married Josephine.
    1045   iii.   Mary Thayer, born 11 July 1821.

Children of Henry Thayer and Betsey Hall are:
    1046   i.   Ansley[8] Thayer.
    1047   ii.   Henry Thayer, born 14 March 1831.
    1048   iii.   Marvin Thayer, born 19 August 1832.

814. Ziba[7] Cook (Joanna[6] Darling, Samuel[5], Samuel[4], Captain John[3], Denice[2], George[1]) was born 22 February 1791. He married **Sally Cook** 1813, daughter of Esek Cook and Thankful Whipple. She was born 04 December 1792 in Pelham, Massachusetts.

Children of Ziba Cook and Sally Cook are:

| 1049 | i. | Silas[8] Cook, born 1814 in Pelham, Massachusetts. |
| 1050 | ii. | Lavina Cook, born 1835. She married Albert Lyman Draper 04 July 1848 in Pelham, Massachusetts; born 183. |

815. Miranda[7] Cook (Joanna[6] Darling, Samuel[5], Samuel[4], Captain John[3], Denice[2], George[1]) was born 09 April 1793, and died 30 July 1887. She married **Stephen Cook** 06 April 1822, son of Aaron Cook and Rachel Clark. He was born 1782 in Wrentham, Massachusetts, and died 21 May 1862 in Wrentham, Massachusetts.

Children of Miranda Cook and Stephen Cook are:

1051	i.	James[8] Cook born 15 April 1823 in Wrentham, Massachusetts; died 26 July 1885 in UNMARRIED.
1052	ii.	Lucie E. Cook, born 27 March 1825 in Wrentham, Massachusetts. She married Samuel Esten 20 March 1846.
1053	iii.	Sena Ann Cook, born 1828. She married Nathan Aldrich Cook.
1054	iv.	Lucius Olney Cook born 1831.
1055	v.	Olive Cook, born 1832.
1056	vi.	Stillman R. Cook, born 01 December 1834 in Wrentham, Massachusetts. He married Mary Fenton.

818. Reuben[7] Cook (Joanna[6] Darling, Samuel[5], Samuel[4], Captain John[3], Denice[2], George[1]) was born 27 December 1776 in Cumberland, Rhode Island, and died 06 March 1867 in Bellingham, Massachusetts. He married **Martha Whipple** 25 April 1802 in Cumberland, Rhode Island, daughter of Simon Whipple and Lavina Staples. She was born 20 June 1779 in Cumberland, Rhode Island, and died 28 May 1828 in Bellingham, Massachusetts.

Children of Reuben Cook and Martha Whipple are:

| + | 1057 | i. | Elias[8] Cook, born 24 August 1802 in Cumberland, Rhode Island; died 11 September 1890 in Boston, Massachusetts. |
| + | 1058 | ii. | Lyman Arnold Cook, born 17 March 1804 in Cumberland, Rhode Island; died 15 July 1873 in Woonsocket, Rhode Island. |

+	1059	iii.	Almira Cook, born 25 April 1805 in Cumberland, Rhode Island; died 02 February 1860 in Bellingham, Massachusetts.
+	1060	iv.	Diadema Cook, born 05 May 1808 in Bellingham, Massachusetts.
	1061	v.	Mary Ann W. Cook, born 22 January 1810 in Bellingham, Massachusetts; died 24 June 1876. She married Benjamin Foster 22 June 1836.
	1062	vi.	Alpha Cook, born 28 July 1813 in Bellingham, Massachusetts; died 11 November 1878. She married (1) Fenner Cook; born 14 May 1802 in Cumberland, Rhode Island. She married (2) Welcome B. Darling 28 January 1832; born 1809.
	1063	vii.	Reuben Olney Cook, born 18 June 1822 in Bellingham, Massachusetts. He married Lydia A. Martin in Rehoboth, Massachusetts.

822. Asa[7] Darling (Samuel[6], Samuel[5], Samuel[4], Captain John[3], Denice[2], George[1]) was born 18 July 1783 in Bellingham, Massachusetts, and died 16 July 1819 in Bellingham, Massachusetts. He married **Julia Thayer** 10 June 1810. She was born 07 August 1768 in Franklin, Massachusetts, and died 24 March 1879.

Child of Asa Darling and Julia Thayer is:
| | 1064 | i. | Asa[8] Darling, born 24 January 1813; died 10 April 1876. He married Sylvia Leland 03 December 1838. |

825. Rhoda[7] Darling (Samuel[6], Samuel[5], Samuel[4], Captain John[3], Denice[2], George[1]) was born 28 May 1789 in Bellingham, Massachusetts, and died March 1854 He committed SUICIDE. She married **Elias Chapin** 30 December 1814 in Providence, Rhode Island. He was born 19 March 1790 in Milford, Massachusetts.

Children of Rhoda Darling and Elias Chapin are:
| | 1065 | i. | Charles[8] Chapin, born 06 March 1816 in Milford, Massachusetts. |
| | 1066 | ii. | Maria Chapin, born 02 February 1818 in Milford, Massachusetts. |

1067	iii.	Hollis Chapin, born 12 December 1819 in Milford, Massachusetts.
1068	iv.	Cyrus Chapin, born 16 March 1822 in Milford, Massachusetts.

827. Samuel[7] Darling (Samuel[6], Samuel[5], Samuel[4], Captain John[3], Denice[2], George[1]) was born 14 August 1793 in Bellingham, Massachusetts, and died 1874. He married **(1) Julia/Judith Morse** He married **(2) Margaret Smith** 28 May 1815 in Bellingham, Massachusetts. She was born 1797, and died 1847 in Bellingham, Massachusetts.

Child of Samuel Darling and Julia/Judith Morse is:

1069	i.	Lyman Morse[8] Darling, born 05 May 1850 in Bellingham, Massachusetts.

Children of Samuel Darling and Margaret Smith are:

1070	i.	George[8] Darling, born 15 August 1815 in Bellingham, Massachusetts. He married Abigail Rockwood 13 March 1836 in Bellingham, Massachusetts.
1071	ii.	Charles Darling, born 21 July 1817 in Bellingham, Massachusetts; died 31 January 1835 in Bellingham, Massachusetts.

Notes for Charles Darling
Charles Darling is buried at the Center Cemetery, located on Rte 140 in Bellingham, Massachusetts

1072	iii.	Gilbert Darling, born 21 January 1819 in Bellingham, Massachusetts; died 01 January 1898.
+ 1073	iv.	Samuel Darling, born 02 March 1825 in Bellingham, Massachusetts; died 1898.
+ 1074	v.	Lucius Darling, born 03 October 1827 in Bellingham, Massachusetts; died 03 January 1896.
1075	vi.	Ruel Darling, born 03 May 1830 in Bellingham, Massachusetts.
+ 1076	vii.	Edwin Darling, born 14 June 1834 in Bellingham, Massachusetts; died 30 September 1898.

832. Jefferson Burr[7] Darling (Samuel[6], Samuel[5], Samuel[4], Captain John[3], Denice[2], George[1]) was born 02 May 1803 in

Bellingham, Massachusetts, and died 10 July 1882 in Bellingham, Massachusetts. He married **Joanna Smith** 27 May 1823 in Bellingham, Massachusetts. She was born 29 August 1803 in Bellingham, Massachusetts, and died 06 January 1880 in Bellingham, Massachusetts.

Notes for Jefferson Burr Darling:
Jefferson Burr Darling and his wife Joanna Smith are buried at the Union Cemetery, located on Route 140 in Bellingham, Massachusetts

Children of Jefferson Darling and Joanna Smith are:

1077 i. Mary Ann[8] Darling, born 08 April 1824 in Bellingham, Massachusetts. She married Levi P. Colburn 24 November 1842 in Bellingham, Massachusetts.

1078 ii. William Wallace Darling, born 02 March 1829 in Bellingham, Massachusetts.

1079 iii. Mayo Cook Darling, born 12 January 1830 in Bellingham, Massachusetts.

1080 iv. Sarah Augusta Darling, born 09 August 1836 in Bellingham, Massachusetts; died 25 November 1858 in Bellingham, Massachusetts.

> Notes for Sarah Augusta Darling:
> Sarah Augusta Darling is buried at the Union Cemetery, located on Rte 140 in Bellingham, Massachusetts

1081 v. Edwin Darling, born 23 July 1826 in Bellingham, Massachusetts; died 21 October 1828 in Bellingham, Massachusetts.

> Notes for Edwin Darling:
> Edwin Darling is also buried at the Union Cemetery

839. John Adams[7] Darling (Ziba[6], Samuel[5], Samuel[4], Captain John[3], Denice[2], George[1]) was born 15 May 1802 in Providence, Rhode Island, and died 14 July 1879 in Providence, Rhode Island. He married **Eliza Potter** 09 August 1824, daughter of Henry Potter and Mary. She was born 30 November 1794 in South Kingstown, Rhode Island, and died 10 September 1868.

Children of John Darling and Eliza Potter are:
- 1082   i.   John Quincy Adams[8] Darling, born 28 February 1825; died 02 April 1826.
- + 1083   ii.   George Henry Darling, born 26 August 1827 in Providence, Rhode Island; died 27 April 1897.
- 1084   iii.   Mary Elizabeth Darling, born 14 November 182[7]; died 29 November 1848.

843. Willis[7] Cook (Rhoda[6] Darling, Samuel[5], Samuel[4], Captain John[3], Denice[2], George[1]) was born 05 September 1803 in Cumberland, Rhode Island, and died 11 February 1882. He married **Cyrene Thayer** 03 July 1828, daughter of Moses Thayer and Ann Paine. She was born 11 September 1808, and died 18 January 1891.

More About Willis Cook:
Willis Cook and his wife Cyrene Thayer are buried at the Oak Hill Cemetery, located on Rathbun Street in Woonsocket, Rhode Island

Children of Willis Cook and Cyrene Thayer are:
- 1085   i.   Ann Janetta[8] Cook.
- 1086   ii.   Ann Olivia Cook She married John R. Boyden.
- 1087   iii.   Cyrene J. Cook. She married John R. Boyden.
- 1088   iv.   Gertrude Cook.
- 1089   v.   Medora Cook. She married Reuben G. Crandall.
- 1090   vi.   Susan A. Cook. She married Henry L. Ballou
- 1091   vii.   Eliphalet Cook, born 22 March 1829; died 08 March 1886.
- 1092   viii.   Horace C. Cook born 13 November 1830; died 22 January 1873.
- 1093   ix.   Edna L. Cook, born 23 October 1843; died 21 July 1850.

844. Lyman Arnold[7] Cook (Rhoda[6] Darling, Samuel[5], Samuel[4], Captain John[3], Denice[2], George[1]) was born 17 March 1805 in Cumberland, Rhode Island, and died 04 December 1898. He married **(1) Almira B. Cook**, daughter of Davis Cook and Abigail Ballou. She was born 24 February 1810 in Cumberland, Rhode Island, and died 11 February 1897. He married **(2) Lavina**

B. **Smith** 22 September 1830. She was born 22 August 1808, and died 03 August 1883.

More About Lyman Arnold Cook:
Lyman Arnold Cook and his wife Lovina B. Smith are buried at the Oakhill Cemetery, located on Rathbun Street in Woonsocket, Rhode Island

Children of Lyman Cook and Lavina Smith are:

1094   i.   George Smith[8] Cook, born 14 January 1832; died 30 December 1842.

> More About George Smith Cook:
> George Smith Cook is buried at the Oak Hill cemetery, located on Rathbun Steeet in Woonsocket, Rhode Island

1095   ii.   Henry Lyman Cook, born 08 October 1834; died 31 March 1835.

> More About Henry Lyman Cook:
> Henry Lyman Cook is buried at the Oak Hill cemetery, located on Rathbun Street in Woonsocket, Rhode Island

1096   iii. Edward Lyman Cook.

858. Nahum[7] Prentice (Sarah[6] Draper, Jonathan[5], Mary[4] Darling, Captain John[3], Denice[2], George[1]) was born 08 May 1783 in Sutton, Massachusetts. He married **Asenath Thayer** 25 July 1813 daughter of Joseph Thayer and Phebe Cook. She was born 23 July 1782 in Mendon, Massachusetts.

Children of Nahum Prentice and Asenath Thayer are:

1097   i.   Louisa May[8] Prentice, born 04 July 1813 in New York.
1098   ii.   Alfred James Prentice born 19 October 1817

859. Rachel[7] Clark (Molly[6] Draper, Jonathan[5], Mary[4] Darling, Captain John[3], Denice[2], George[1]) was born 03 August 1792, and died 09 March 1865. She married **Anson Cook** 20 April 1816, son of Aaron Cook and Rachel Clark. He was born 10

April 1792 in Wrentham, Massachusetts, and died 25 September 1873·

More About Rachel Clark:
Rachel Clark and her husband Anson Cook are buried at the Rakeville Cemetery, located on Lake Street in Bellingham, Massachusetts

Children of Rachel Clark and Anson Cook are:
1099	i.	Eddy Clark[8] Cook, born 1817.
1100	ii.	Aaron Clark Cook born 27 June 1819 in Bellingham, Massachusetts; died 02 September 1844 UNMARRIED.
1101	iii.	Rachel Cook, born 25 April 1822. She married Jarvis Cass.
1102	iv.	Elizabeth Jillson Cook, born June 1824. She married William A. Clark.
1103	v.	Anson Eddy Cook· born 15 May 1826 died 1901 UNMARRIED.
1104	vi.	Mary Maria Cook, born 18 August 1829.
1105	vii.	Susan Ann Cook, born 26 March 1831; died 26 June 1889. She married Samuel Wilcox.

860. Ahimaz[7] Darling (Ahimaaz[6], Joshua[5], Samuel[4], Captain John[3], Denice[2], George[1]) died 05 September 1874 in Bellingham, Massachusetts. He married **Margaretta Chilson** 13 April 1828 in Bellingham, Massachusetts. She died 17 January 1886 in Bellingham, Massachusetts.

Notes for Ahimaz Darling:
Ahimaz Darling and his wife Margaretta Chilson are both buried at the Rakeville Cemetery, located on Lake Street in Bellingham, Massachusetts

Children of Ahimaz Darling and Margaretta Chilson are:
1106	i.	Ahimaz[8] Darling, born 11 June 1829 in Bellingham, Massachusetts.
1107	ii.	William Addison Darling, born 23 March 1838 in Bellingham, Massachusetts.

861. Eliza[7] Wilson (Benjamin[6], Penelope[5] Darling, Samuel[4], Captain John[3], Denice[2], George[1]) was born 09 April 1808, and died 29 November 1853 in Willet, New York. She married **Burr Livermore** 30 January 1832 in German, New York, son of Abel Livermore and Deborah Salisbury. He was born 28 October 1810 in German, New York, and died 05 September 1878 in Earlville, New York.

Children of Eliza Wilson and Burr Livermore are:

+   1108   i.   Elvira Wilson[8] Livermore, born 12 April 1834 in German, New York.

    1109   ii.   Benjamin Wesley Livermore, born 04 October 1838 in Willet, New York; died 20 June 1868 in Stika, Alaska.

            Notes for Benjamin Wesley Livermore:

            2nd Lt. in Indiana Artillery (Megis' Barrery) during the Civil War. Was Officer of the day in Sitka, Alaska when the Russian flag was lowered and the Stars and Stripes were raised. Killed by an accidental discharge of a Henry Rifle.

    1110   iii.   Miles Livermore, born 03 October 1842 in Cincinnatus, New York; died 19 November 1861.

    1111   iv.   Giles Livermore, born 03 October 1842 in Cincinnatus, New York; died 06 November 1861.

+   1112   v.   Eliza Janet Livermore, born 07 November 1844 in Cincinnatus, New York; died 10 February 1896 in Norwich, New York.

    1113   vi.   Will... elbert Livermore, born 10 October 1851 in Willet, New York; died in DeKalb, Illinois.

874. Henry[7] Allen (Asenath[6] Colman, Susannah[5] Martin, John[4], Hannah[3] Darling, Denice[2], George[1]) was born 15 May 1798 in Ashby, Massachusetts, and died 13 February 1885 in East Wallingfard, Vermont. He married **Sally Constantine** 25 March 1825, daughter of Jacob Constantine. She died 22 August 1800 in East Wallingfard, Vermont.

Children of Henry Allen and Sally Constantine are:

1114	i.	James Tenney[8] Allen, born 13 March 1827 in Nottingham; died 02 March 1834 in Ashby, Massachusetts.
+ 1115	ii.	George Franklin Allen, born 01 April 1830 in Ashby, Massachusetts.
1116	iii.	Caroline Augusta Allen, born 28 June 1833 in Ashby, Massachusetts; died 11 September 1836 in Townsand, Massachusetts.
+ 1117	iv.	James Charles Mansfield Allen, born 30 January 1836 in Townsand, Massachusetts.
1118	v.	Henry C. Allen, born 05 April 1843 in Fitchburg, Massachusetts; died 02 June 1862 in Savage Station, Virginia.

More About Henry C. Allen:
Henry C. Allen was a Private in Co. C Fifth Vermont Volunteer Infantry...Killed in action

+ 1119	vi.	Otis Jewett Allen, born 17 June 1846 in Fitchburg, Massachusetts; died 08 January 1885 in Whitehall, Wisconsin.
1120	vii.	Andrew Allen, died in INFANCY.
1121	viii.	Asenath Colman Allen, born 18 October 1848 in Winchendon, Massachusetts. She married Harrison Gilliland 04 September 1873 in Whitehall, Wisconsin; born 19 October 1837 in Hamilton Township, Jackson County, Ohio
1122	ix.	Willie Allen

876. Louisa[7] Allen (Asenath[6] Colman, Susannah[5] Martin, John[4], Hannah[3] Darling, Denice[2], George[1]) was born 24 September 1801 in Ashby, Massachusetts, and died 31 January 1874 in Newton, Massachusetts. She married **Henry Blodgett** 02 December 1827. He was born 17 March 1801 in Colbrook, New Hampshire, and died 19 July 1890.

Children of Louisa Allen and Henry Blodgett are:

+ 1123	i.	Ann Louisa[8] Blodgett, born 01 November 1828 in Boston, Massachusetts; died 16 April 1895.
1124	ii.	Benjamin Colman Blodgett, born 31 May 1834 in Boston, Massachusetts; died 04 October 1837.
1125	iii.	Benjamin Colman Blodgett, born 12 March 1838 in Boston, Massachusetts.

1126   iv.   William Henry Blodgett, born 08 January 1841 in Boston, Massachusetts.

1127   v.   Frances Amelia Blodgett, born 06 December 1844 in Boston, Massachusetts.

894. Maria^7 Darling (Elisha^6, Job^5, Samuel^4, Daniel^3, Denice^2, George^1) was born 1808 in Burrillville, Rhode Island, and died 08 December 1861 in Burrillville, Rhode Island. She married **William Smith Darling** 04 October 1840 in Smithfield, Rhode Island, son of Henry Darling and Mary Wilbur. He was born 02 June 1808 in Smithfield, Rhode Island.

Child of Maria Darling and William Darling is:

1128   i.   Smith Walling^8 Darling, born 06 May 1842 in Burrillville, Rhode Island; died 12 January 1872. He married Susan Taft 02 January 1869 in Burrillville, Rhode Island; born 1844 in Burrillville, Rhode Island.

907. James Edmond^7 Darling (Lyman^6, Benson^5, Samuel^4, Daniel^3, Denice^2, George^1) was born 1843 in Medfield, Massachusetts. He married **Clara Emma Inman** 08 April 1873 in Mendon, Massachusetts. She was born 1853 in Mendon, Massachusetts.

Children of James Darling and Clara Inman are:

1129   i.   Floyd Everett^8 Darling, born 15 July 1876 in Mendon, Massachusetts.

1130   ii.   James Edmond Darling, born 18 February 1877 in Mendon, Massachusetts.

917. Moses Oscar^7 Darling (Artemus^6, Benson^5, Samuel^4, Daniel^3, Denice^2, George^1) was born 07 August 1841 in Mendon, Massachusetts, and died 05 March 1891 in Johnston, Rhode Island. He married **Martha Ann Gordon** 20 June 1864 in Providence, Rhode Island. She died 05 March 1940.

Notes for Moses Oscar Darling:

Moses Oscar Darling is buried at the Swan Point Cemetery, located on Blackstone Blvd. In Providence, Rhode Island

More About Martha Ann Gordon:
Martha Ann Gordon is also buried at the Swan Point Cemetery, Providence, Rhode Island

Children of Moses Darling and Martha Gordon are:

1131   i.   Walter Eugene[8] Darling, born 25 May 1868 in Providence, Rhode Island; died 13 August 1868 in Providence, Rhode Island.

1132   ii.   Mabel Bowen Darling, born 23 January 1869 in Providence, Rhode Island; died 27 October 1887 in Providence, Rhode Island.

1133   iii.   Oscar Eugene Darling, born 24 March 1871 in Providence, Rhode Island; died 10 July 1963.

1134   iv.   Mattie Darling, born 04 October 1873 in Providence, Rhode Island; died 20 November 1876 in Providence, Rhode Island.

1135   v.   Irving Taft Darling, born 13 December 1877 in Johnston, Rhode Island; died 19 March 1897 in Providence, Rhode Island.

918. Joseph[7] Sprague (Mary Susan[6] Taft, Jemima[5] Thompson, Susannah[4] Darling, Daniel[3], Denice[2], George[1]) was born 29 April 1796 in Huntington, Vermont, and died 19 December 1875. He married **Lucy Thomas**. She was born 26 November 1794 in Huntington, Vermont, and died 12 May 1879.

Children of Joseph Sprague and Lucy Thomas are:

1136   i.   David Daniel[8] Sprague, born 16 November 1828 in Huntington, Vermont; died 10 August 1915 in Hinesburg, Vermont He married Mary Ann Sweet 02 February 1851 in Huntington, Vermont; born 1834; died 1898.

1137   ii.   John T. Sprague, born 28 December 1824; died 12 January 1911. He married Rosetta Douglas; born 1828; died 1893.

1138   iii.   Rebecca Sprague. She married Justin Sweet.

1139   iv.   Stephen M. Sprague, born 1833; died 1889. He married Sarah M. Lewis; born 1833 died 1914

1140   v.   Heman Sprague, born 1835; died 11 April 1876. He married Roselfa Ross 24 December 1857; born 1839; died 1885.

1141   vi.   Sarah Sprague, born 1836. She married Ovet Hullock 1857.
1142   vii. Levina Sprague. She married Henry Sweet.

919. Gideon[7] Sprague (Mary Susan[6] Taft, Jemima[5]
Thompson, Susannah[4] Darling, Daniel[3], Denice[2], George[1]) was
born 1806 in Wallingford, Vermont, and died 12 December 1884
in Huntington, Vermont. He married **Sally Taft**, daughter of
Gideon Taft. She was born 1818 in Wallingford, Vermont, and
died 22 April 1889 in Huntingto, Vermont

Children of Gideon Sprague and Sally Taft are:
1143   i.   Sylvester[8] Sprague, born 1841.
1144   ii.   Mary G. Sprague.
1145   iii. Mercy Sprague, born 24 August 1842.
1146   iv. Emerson Sprague.
1147   v.   Julia Sprague, born 1849.

921. Phineas[7] Sprague (Mary Susan[6] Taft, Jemima[5]
Thompson, Susannah[4] Darling, Daniel[3], Denice[2], George[1]) was
born 1819 in Wallingford, Vermont, and died Abt. 1895 in
Huntingto, Vermont. He married **Emily (Church) Hardy** 09
March 1836. She was born 1819, and died 1894 in Huntingto,
Vermont.

Children of Phineas Sprague and Emily Hardy are:
1148   i.   Enos M.[8] Sprague.
1149   ii.   Jane Sprague born 1838
1150   iii. Henry Sprague, born 1840.
1151   iv. George Sprague, born 1842.
1152   v.   Norman Sprague, born 1845
1153   vi. Mary Sprague, born 1848.
1154   vii. Bently Sprague.

922. Manassah[7] Sprague (Mary Susan[6] Taft, Jemima[5]
Thompson, Susannah[4] Darling, Daniel[3], Denice[2], George[1]), died
07 February 1886 in Horicon, Warren County, New York. He
married **Laura Taft**, daughter of Gideon Taft. She was born 07

March 1793, and died 11 January 1889 in Horicon, Warren County, New York.

Children of Manassah Sprague and Laura Taft are:

1155　　i.　Governor Gallusha[8] Sprague.
1156　　ii.　Sarah Jane Sprague.
1157　　iii.　Lucinda Sprague.
1158　　iv.　Noble Sprague.
1159　　v.　Hiram Sprague.
1160　　vi.　Sirena Sprague.
1161　　vii.　Malissa Sprague.
1162　　viii.　Susannah Sprague.
1163　　ix.　Mary Sprague.

937. Eleanor[7] Darling (Zelek[6], Zeleck[5], William[4], Daniel[3], Denice[2], George[1]) was born 23 September 1820 in Providence, Rhode Island. She married **William Crooker**.

Child of Eleanor Darling and William Crooker is:

+　1164　　i.　Flora C.[8] Crooker, born 10 October 1845.

940. Sarah[7] Salisbury (Rowena[6] Wheelock, Paul[5], Deborah[4] Darling, Benjamin[3], Denice[2], George[1]). She married **Haley Brown**

Child of Sarah Salisbury and Haley Brown is:

+　1165　　i.　Caroline Lord Salisbury[8] Brown.

943. Lydia[7] Salisbury (Rowena[6] Wheelock, Paul[5], Deborah[4] Darling, Benjamin[3], Denice[2], George[1]) was born 03 September 1788, and died 11 August 1837. He married **Chauncey Smith** September 1801 in Adams, New York son of David Smith. He was born 18 February 1777, and died 02 September 1854.

Children of Lydia Salisbury and Chauncey Smith are:

1166　　i.　Rowena Wheelock[8] Smith born 05 May 1803 in Adams, New York; died 05 April 1885. She married Joseph Allen 20 March 1823.

1167	ii.	Caroline Lord Smith, born 25 June 1805 in Adams, New York; died 12 December 1862. She married (1) Marenus Matthews. She married (2) ——Maltby.
1168	iii.	Chauncey Smith, born 22 February 1807; died 1899. He married (1) Adeline Carpenter. He married (2) Maria.
1169	iv.	Willard Smith born 19 December 1809 died 1810.
1170	v.	Ursula Hawley Smith, born 24 January 1811; died December 1814.
1171	vi.	Sarah Wawkins Smith, born 01 December 1812 in Adams, New York. She married Peter Halmer Turner 28 September 1858.
+ 1172	vii.	Lydia Ann Smith, born 20 January 1815 in Adams, New York; died 26 March 1858.
1173	viii.	Adelibe DeMontall Smith, born 24 February 1817 in Adams, New York. She married Thomas Hamilton 13 May 1836.
1174	ix.	Jane Antoinette Smith, born 03 March 1819 in Adams, New York; died August 1862. She married J.R. Bates 1839.
1175	x.	Clarinda A. Smith, born 12 August 1821; died 03 September 1837.

946. Seneca Sales[7] Salisbury (Rowena[6] Wheelock, Paul[5], Deborah[4] Darling, Benjamin[3], Denice[2], George[1]) was born 1794, and died 1889 in Clayton, Kansas. He married **Sallie/Sarah King**. She was born ca. 10 July 1805 in New York, and died 16 December 1860 in Ellison, Illinois

Child of Seneca Salisbury and Sallie/Sarah King is:
| + 1176 | i. | Allen[8] Salisbury, born 23 December 1832 in Woodstock, Ohio; died 23 February 1884 in Fairmount, Nebraska. |

948. Margery[7] Darling (Thomas Jefferson[6], Jacob[5], Joseph[4], Benjamin[3], Denice[2], George[1]) was born 1807. She married **John Taylor** 02 March 1836. He was born 1799 in England.

Children of Margery Darling and John Taylor are:
1177	i.	Ann[8] Taylor.
1178	ii.	Sopia Taylor.
1179	iii.	George Taylor.
1180	iv.	Hannah Taylor.

973. Esseck[7] Darling (Darius[6], Ebenezer[5], Ebenezer[4], Benjamin[3], Denice[2], George[1]) was born 1808 in Glocester, Rhode Island, and died 24 July 1889 in Woodstock, Connecticut. He married **Rizpah Taft** 06 October 1839 in Burrillville, Rhode Island, daughter of Nathan Taft. She was born 1812, and died 03 May 1893 in Woodstock, Connecticut.

Children of Esseck Darling and Rizpah Taft are:

+   1181   i.   Albert[8] Darling, born 01 April 1843 in Burrillville, Rhode Island; died 27 March 1928 in Connecticut.
+   1182   ii.   Ursula Darling, born July 1841 in Burrillville, Rhode Island; died 1927 in Burrillville, Rhode Island.

974. Nelson[7] Darling (Darius[6], Ebenezer[5], Ebenezer[4], Benjamin[3], Denice[2], George[1]) was born October 1828 in Glocester, Rhode Island, and died 20 December 1878 in Glocester, Rhode Island. He married **(1) Clarissa Bowen** 28 June 1851, daughter of Cyrel Bowen and Ruth Inman. She was born 01 June 1824 in Glocester, Rhode Island, and died 22 April 1857 in Glocester, Rhode Island. He married **(2) Fidelia Bowen** 18 June 1868 in Glocester, Rhode Island, daughter of Harris Bowen and Mary Shippee. She was born 1829 in Glocester, Rhode Island, and died 30 July 1883 in Glocester, Rhode Island.

Notes for Nelson Darling:
Nelson Darling was a Private in the Civil War in the 5th Regiment Rhode Island Heavy Artillery 1861-1863

Notes for Fidelia Bowen:
Fidelia Bowen died as a result of being struck by lightening

Children of Nelson Darling and Clarissa Bowen are:

   1183   i.   Amey[8] Darling, born 14 September 1851 in Glocester, Rhode Island; died 07 March 1869 in Glocester, Rhode Island.
   1184   ii.   Martha Salone Darling, born 25 July 1854 in Glocester, Rhode Island; died 13 May 1855 in Glocester, Rhode Island.

1185   iii.   Ora Weston Darling, born 05 May 1856 in Glocester, Rhode Island. He married Emma Balmforth; born 24 June 1859 in Greenville, Rhode Island.

977. Angell[7] Darling (William[6], Ebenezer[5], Ebenezer[4], Benjamin[3], Denice[2], George[1]) was born 1797 in Glocester, Rhode Island. He married **Lucy Page**, daughter of Joseph Page and Freelove Keach. She was born in Glocester, Rhode Island.

Children of Angell Darling and Lucy Page are:
1186   i.   Angell[8] Darling, born 1830 in Glocester, Rhode Island.
1187   ii.   Anne Frances Darling, born 1833 in Glocester, Rhode Island; died 04 February 1897 in Burrillville, Rhode Island.

978. Sarah Ann[7] Darling (William[6], Ebenezer[5], Ebenezer[4], Benjamin[3], Denice[2], George[1]) was born 28 August 1798 in Glocester, Rhode Island, and died 05 April 1885 in Glocester, Rhode Island. She married **George Sprague** son of Elijah Sprague and Anna Sprague. He was born 03 July 1788 in Glocester, Rhode Island, and died 19 February 1879 in Glocester, Rhode Island.

Notes for George Sprague:
George Sprague was a farmer. He died of Pneumouia....

Children of Sarah Darling and George Sprague are:
1188   i.   Amanda[8] Sprague, born 1822.
1189   ii.   Francis Sprague, born 1825.
1190   iii.   Caroline Sprague, born 1828.

980. Riley[7] Darling (William[6], Ebenezer[5], Ebenezer[4], Benjamin[3], Denice[2], George[1]) was born 09 September 1810 in Glocester, Rhode Island, and died 25 January 1907 in East Greenwich, Rhode Island. He married **Patience Arnold**, daughter of David Arnold and Polly Cutler. She was born in Glocester, Rhode Island.

Children of Riley Darling and Patience Arnold are:
1191   i.   Ellen Maria[8] Darling.
1192   ii. Eliza Darling.
1193   iii. Francis Darling, born 1840.

988. William Smith[7] Darling (Henry[6], Henry[5], Samuel[4], Benjamin[3], Denice[2], George[1]) was born 02 June 1808 in Smithfield, Rhode Island. He married **Maria Darling** 04 October 1840 in Smithfield, Rhode Island, daughter of Elisha Darling and Ruth Walling. She was born 1808 in Burrillville, Rhode Island, and died 08 December 1861 in Burrillville, Rhode Island.

Child is listed above under (894) Maria Darling

Generation No. 7

1032. George[8] Darling (John[7], Phineas[6], Pelatiah[5], John[4], Captain John[3], Denice[2], George[1]) was born 05 May 1840 in Burrillville, Rhode Island. He married **Cynthia White** 1862 in Burrillville, Rhode Island. She died 1894.

Child of George Darling and Cynthia White is:
1194   i.   Carrie B.[9] Darling

1033. William[8] Darling (John[7], Phineas[6], Pelatiah[5], John[4], Captain John[3], Denice[2], George[1]) was born 29 September 1844 in Burrillville, Rhode Island, and died 21 August 1886 in Burrillville, Rhode Island. He married **Annie Clark**.

Children of William Darling and Annie Clark are:
1195   i.   Minnie E.[9] Darling She married Wallace Putnam.
1196   ii. Sadie B. Darling
1197   iii. Susan H. Darling. She married Carl Putnam.
1198   iv. William E. Darling, died 07 December 1895.

1199   v.   Amos Darling, born 13 September 1846. He married
Rebecca Ellen Jencks.

1035. Esek[8] Darling (John[7], Phineas[6], Pelatiah[5], John[4], Captain John[3], Denice[2], George[1]) was born 13 September 1842. He married **(1) Jane Waterhouse** 1862 in England. She was born in England. He married **(2) Sarah Waterhouse** 1866 in Burrillville, Rhode Island. She was born in England.

More About Esek Darling:
Esek Darling served in the Civil War in the 7th Rhode Island Infantry

Children of Esek Darling and Sarah Waterhouse are:
    1200   i.   John L.[9] Darling.
    1201   ii.   Etta Darling.
    1202 iii.   Dora Darling.
    1203 iv.   Theodore Darling.

1036. Labin[8] Thayer (Hannah[7] Taft, Nahum[6], Priscilla[5] Thayer, Ruth[4] Darling, Captain John[3], Denice[2], George[1]) was born 09 February 1793. He married **Abigail Thayer** 25 January 1815.

Children of Labin Thayer and Abigail Thayer are:
    1204   i.   Rachel[9] Thayer, born 02 December 1816.
    1205   ii.   Adelaide Thayer, born 01 December 1819
+   1206 iii.   Sumner Thayer, born November 1822.

1038. Pelatiah[8] Thayer (Hannah[7] Taft, Nahum[6], Priscilla[5] Thayer, Ruth[4] Darling, Captain John[3], Denice[2], George[1]) was born 03 January 1800 in Mendon, Massachusetts, and died 07 October 1849 in Bellingham, Massachusetts   He married **Alsee Adams** 15 August 1824 in Bellingham, Massachusetts.

Children of Pelatiah Thayer and Alsee Adams are:
    1207   i.   Clarissa Adams[9] Thayer, born 20 September 182

1208	ii.	Hannah Rebecca Thayer, born 16 June 1826 in Bellingham, Massachusetts.
1209	iii.	Albert H. Thayer, born 04 October 1830.
1210	iv.	Pelatiah Thayer, born 18 February 1836 in Mendon, Massachusetts.

1041. Artemus[8] Thayer (Hannah[7] Taft, Nahum[6], Priscilla[5] Thayer, Ruth[4] Darling, Captain John[3], Denice[2], George[1]) was born 1813, and died 1888. He married **Sylvia Thayer** 18 March 1838 in Mendon, Massachusetts, daughter of Ariel Thayer and Lydia White. She was born 17 October 1817 in Mendon, Massachusetts, and died 1910.

Notes for Artemus Thayer:

Artemus Thayer, his wife Sylvia Thayer, and their children, Clara, William and Walter are all buried at the Pine Hill Cemetery, located on Providence Road in Mendon, Massachusetts

Children of Artemus Thayer and Sylvia Thayer are:

	1211	i.	Clara E.[9] Thayer, born 1846; died 1847
	1212	ii.	William Thayer, born 1848; died 1871.
	1213	iii.	Walter J. Thayer, born 1856; died 1866.
+	1214	iv.	Edwin Lambert Thayer, born 03 November 1840.
+	1215	v.	George H. Thayer, born 10 October 1844.
	1216	vi.	Clarissa E. Thayer, born 22 January 1846.
	1217	vii.	Elmer James Thayer, born 29 January 1852; died 08 September 1857.
	1218	viii.	Walter Grovenor Thayer born 22 September 1856 died 16 September 1857.

1043. George Washington[8] Thayer (Henry[7], Peter[6], Peter[5], Ruth[4] Darling, Captain John[3], Denice[2], George[1]) was born 28 February 1817 .He married **Candance Rising**.

Children of George Thayer and Candance Rising are:

| 1219 | i. | George Henry[9] Thayer. |
| 1220 | ii. | Cyrene E. Thayer. |

1057. Elias[8] Cook (Reuben[7], Joanna[6] Darling, Samuel[5], Samuel[4], Captain John[3], Denice[2], George[1]) was born 24 August 1802 in Cumberland, Rhode Island, and died 11 September 1890 in Boston, Massachusetts. He married **Orinda B. Gaskill** 17 July 1824. She was born 1800, and died 1868.

More About Elias Cook:
Elias Cook and his wife Orinda B. Gaskill are both buried at the Oak Hill Cemetery, located on Rathbun Street in Woonsocket, Rhode Island

Child of Elias Cook and Orinda Gaskill is:
1221   i.   Elias S.[9] Cook, born 1825; died 1862

> More About Elias S. Cook:
> Elias S. Cook is also buried at the Oak Hill Cemetery, located on Rathbun Street in Woonsocket, Rhode Island

1058. Lyman Arnold[8] Cook (Reuben[7], Joanna[6] Darling, Samuel[5], Samuel[4], Captain John[3], Denice[2], George[1]) was born 17 March 1804 in Cumberland, Rhode Island, and died 15 July 1873 in Woonsocket, Rhode Island. He married **Almira B. Cook** 12 April 1839, daughter of Davis Cook and Abigail Ballou. She was born 24 February 1810 in Cumberland, Rhode Island, and died 11 February 1897.

More About Lyman Arnold Cook:
Lyman Arnold Cook is buried at the Rhode Island Historical Cemetery # 2, located on Cumberland Hill Road, in Woonsocket, Rhode Island

More About Almira B. Cook:
Almira B. Cook is buried at the Rhode Island Historical Cemetery # 2, Cumberland Hill Road, Woonsocket, Rhode Island

Children of Lyman Cook and Almira Cook are:

1222   i.   S. Jennie[9] Cook, born 21 July 1846; died 25 June 1892. She married Frederick A. Ingerson

           More About S. Jennie Cook:
           Jennie Cook is buried at the Rhode Island Historical Cemetery # 2, located on Cumberland Hill Road, in Woonsocket, Rhode Island

1223   ii.   Samantha B. Cook, born 03 May 1831; died 14 May 1832.

           More About Samantha B. Cook:
           Samatha B. Cook is buried at the Rhode Island Historical Cemetery # 2, located on Cumberland Hill Road, in Woonsocket, Rhode Island

1224   iii.   Lucina S. Cook, born 25 July 1835; died 04 March 1841.

           More About Lucina S. Cook:
           Lucina Cook is bured at the Rhode Island Historical Cemetery # 2, located on Cumberland Hill Road, in Woonsocket, Rhode Island

1225   iv.   Ann Eliza Cook, born 16 January 1838; died 23 August 1838.

           More About Ann Eliza Cook:
           Ann Eliza Cook is bured at the Rhode Island Historical Cemetery # 2, located on Cumberland Hill Road, in Woonsocket, Rhode Island

1226   v.   Ellen M. Cook, born 16 December 1842; died 14 May 1844.

           More About Ellen M. Cook:
           Ellen Cook is buried at the: Rhode Island Historical Cemetery # 2, located on Cumberland Hill Road, in Woonsocket, Rhode Island

1059. Almira[8] Cook (Reuben[7], Joanna[6] Darling, Samuel[5], Samuel[4], Captain John[3], Denice[2], George[1]) was born 25 April 1805 in Cumberland, Rhode Island, and died 02 February 1860 in Bellingham, Massachusetts. She married **John Chison** 29

November 1823 in Bellingham, Massachusetts. He was born 25 October 1790 in Bellingham, Massachusetts

Children of Almira Cook and John Chison are:

1227   i.   John Draper[9] Chison, born 29 October 1824.

1228   ii.   Lucius Addison Chison, born 31 May 1830.

1060. Diadema[8] Cook (Reuben[7], Joanna[6] Darling, Samuel[5], Samuel[4], Captain John[3], Denice[2], George[1]) was born 05 May 1808 in Bellingham, Massachusetts. She married **Orrin Chilson** 13 March 1825 in Franklin, Massachusetts. He was born 25 July 1799 in Bellingham, Massachusetts.

Children of Diadema Cook and Orrin Chilson are:

1229   i.   Martha Whipple[9] Chilson, born 20 March 1826 in Bellingham, Massachusetts.

1230   ii.   Reuben Chilson, born 13 October 1828 in Bellingham, Massachusetts; died 1916. He married Hannah J. Cook born 1834; died 1905.

         More About Reuben Chilson:
         Reuben Chilson and his wife Hannah Cook are buried at the Rhode Island Historical Cemetery # 2, located on Cumberland Hill Road, in Woonsocket, Rhode Island

1231   iii.   Orrin Chilson, born 06 October 1830 in Bellingham, Massachusetts.

1232   iv.   Diadama Cook Chilson, born 23 October 1832 in Bellingham, Massachusetts.

1233   v.   Libbeus Chilson, born 01 March 1835 in Bellingham, Massachusetts.

1234   vi.   James Olney Chilson, born 28 March 1837 in Bellingham, Massachusetts.

1235   vii.   Lewis Morton Chilson, born 1842.

1236   viii.   Mary E. Chilson, born 1846.

1237   ix.   Eliza Ellen Chilson, born 29 May 1848 in Bellingham, Massachusetts.

1238   x.   Mariana Chilson, born 07 February 1850 in Bellingham, Massachusetts.

1073. Samuel[8] Darling (Samuel[7], Samuel[6], Samuel[5], Samuel[4], Captain John[3], Denice[2], George[1]) was born 02 March 1825 in Bellingham, Massachusetts, and died 1898. He married **Emily Adams** 26 May 1846, daughter of Joseph Adams and Asenath Partridge. She was born 05 December 1826 in Bellingham, Massachusetts.

Children of Samuel Darling and Emily Adams are:

1239	i.	Edmund Adams[9] Darling, born 18 January 1849.
1240	ii.	Walter Emerson Darling, born 23 November 1854.
1241	iii.	Ida Elizabeth Darling, born 26 September 1857.

1074. Lucius[8] Darling (Samuel[7], Samuel[6], Samuel[5], Samuel[4], Captain John[3], Denice[2], George[1]) was born 03 October 1827 in Bellingham, Massachusetts, and died 03 January 1896. He married **Angeline Armington** 04 November 1847 in Bellingham, Massachusetts. She was born 1828.

Children of Lucius Darling and Angeline Armington are:

+	1242	i.	Ira C.[9] Darling, born 1856; died 21 July 1891 in Pawtucket, Rhode Island.
	1243	ii.	Mary Evelyn Darling, died in Worcester, Massachusetts. She married John G. Jefferds 1869; born 1841.
+	1244	iii.	Ada E. Darling.
	1245	iv.	Lovinia Darling. She married Charles A. Fales.
	1246	v.	Lucius Bowles Darling, died 03 January 1896 in Pawtucket, Rhode Island.

> More About Lucius Bowles Darling:
> Lucius Darling is buried at the Swan Point Cemetery, located on Blackstone Blvd. in Providence, Rhode Island... He was Governor of Rhode Island

1247	vi.	Byron Darling, died in INFANCY.

1076. Edwin[8] Darling (Samuel[7], Samuel[6], Samuel[5], Samuel[4], Captain John[3], Denice[2], George[1]) was born 14 June 1834 in Bellingham, Massachusetts, and died 30 September 1898. He married **Abby Adams** 27 December 1860, daughter of Ruel

Adams and Julia. She was born 07 April 1835 in Bellingham, Massachusetts, and died 16 November 1874 in Pawtucket, Rhode Island.

Notes for Abby Adams:
Abby Adams is buried at the Center Cemetery, located on Rte 140 in Bellingham, Massachusetts

Children of Edwin Darling and Abby Adams are:

1248	i.	Oscar[9] Darling, born 1860 in Pawtucket, Rhode Island; died 17 January 1860 in Pawtucket, Rhode Island.
1249	ii.	Julia Darling, born 1863 in Pawtucket, Rhode Island; died 31 July 1863 in Pawtucket, Rhode Island.
1250	iii.	Edwin Darling, born 1864 in Pawtucket, Rhode Island; died 26 September 1865 in Pawtucket, Rhode Island.
1251	iv.	Lloyd Darling, born 1866 in Pawtucket, Rhode Island; died 02 September 1887 in Pawtucket, Rhode Island.
1252	v.	Mabel Darling, born 1869 in Pawtucket, Rhode Island; died 1870.

1083. George Henry[8] Darling (John Adams[7], Ziba[6], Samuel[5], Samuel[4], Captain John[3], Denice[2], George[1]) was born 26 August 1827 in Providence, Rhode Island, and died 27 April 1897. He married **Maria Amelia Sweet** 03 June 1850, daughter of Oliver Sweet and Sarah Gould. She was born 04 April 1830, and died 26 February 1904.

Children of George Darling and Maria Sweet are:

1253	i.	Mary Elizabeth[9] Darling, born 12 March 1851. She married William A. Witherbee 06 November 1872.
1254	ii.	John Oliver Darling, born 24 December 1852. He married Mary R. Bosworth 06 July 1880.
1255	iii.	Welcome Ballou Darling, born 30 October 1855; died 31 July 1906. He married Lizetta Pemberton 01 June 1881
1256	iv.	Grace Darling, born 10 January 1861 She married Franklin A. Snow 23 February 1887.
1257	v.	Geroge Curtis Darling, born 18 December 1864 in Providence, Rhode Island.
1258	vi.	Robert Gould Darling, born 03 July 1868; died 28 October 1888.

1108. Elvira Wilson[8] Livermore (Eliza[7] Wilson, Benjamin[6], Penelope[5] Darling, Samuel[4], Captain John[3], Denice[2], George[1]) was born 12 April 1834 in German, New York. She married **Joseph Osmond** 12 January 1862 in Smithville Flats, New York. He was born 18 February 1826 in Bibery, Pennsylvania.

Children of Elvira Livermore and Joseph Osmond are:

1259   i.   Nettie May[9] Osmond, born 03 May 1869 in Norwich, New York; died 07 October 1870 in Norwich, New York.

1260   ii. Eloise Livermore Osmond, born 17 July 1871 in Norwich, New York.

1112. Eliza Janet[8] Livermore (Eliza[7] Wilson, Benjamin[6], Penelope[5] Darling, Samuel[4], Captain John[3], Denice[2], George[1]) was born 07 November 1844 in Cincinnatus, New York, and died 10 February 1896 in Norwich, New York. She married **Robert Foresman** 07 March 1865 in Hamilton, New York.

Children of Eliza Livermore and Robert Foresman are:

1261   i.   Nellie Maud[9] Foresman, born 14 February 1866[1] died 28 March 1884.

1262   ii. Elvira Livermore Foresman, born 10 February 1868. She married Henry Hewitt.

1263   iii. Sally Foresman, born 06 September 1870. She married William McCaw.

1264   iv. Eddy Foresman, born 03 April 1872.

1265   v. Louis Benjamin Foresman, born 06 June 1874.

1115. George Franklin[8] Allen (Henry[7], Asenath[6] Colman, Susannah[5] Martin, John[4], Hannah[3] Darling, Denice[2], George[1]) was born 01 April 1830 in Ashby, Massachusetts. He married **Emeline L. Bradish** 29 November 1849. She was born 04 September 1831 in Rutland, Vermont.

Children of George Allen and Emeline Bradish are:

+ 1266   i.   Emily Lizzie[9] Allen, born 24 September 1850 in Keene, New Hampshire.

1267	ii.	Franklin George Allen, born 01 October 1852 in Keene, New Hampshire. He married (1) Martha Collins October 1877; born 11 March 1864 in Pleasent Grove, Minnesota; died 02 May 1882. He married (2) Rheuamy Allen 15 April 1897.
1268	iii.	Ellen Jane Allen, born 14 May 1855 in Fitchburg, Massachusetts; died 06 September 1855.
1269	iv.	Ella Laura Allen born 20 July 1861 in Worcester, Massachusetts; died 18 September 1861.
1270	v.	Carrie Etta Allen, born 06 July 1865 in Pleasent Grove, Minnesota; died 25 August 1865.
+ 1271	vi.	Harry James Allen, born 04 January 1869 in Chatfield, Minnesota.
1272	vii.	Benjamin Charles Allen, born 24 January 1876 in Pleasent Grove, Minnesota.

1117. James Charles Mansfield[8] Allen (Henry[7], Asenath[6] Colman, Susannah[5] Martin, John[4], Hannah[3] Darling, Denice[2], George[1]) was born 30 January 1836 in Townsand, Massachusetts. He married **Nellie Maria Green** 26 May 1888. She was born 29 July 1861 in Wallingford, Vermont.

More About James Charles Mansfield Allen:
James Charles Mansfield served in the Civil War

Children of James Allen and Nellie Green are:

1273	i.	Bartha May[9] Allen, born 13 October 1890 in East Wallingfard, Vermont.
1274	ii.	Percy Walter Allen, born 26 June 1894 in East Wallingfard, Vermont.

1119. Otis Jewett[8] Allen (Henry[7], Asenath[6] Colman, Susannah[5] Martin, John[4], Hannah[3] Darling, Denice[2], George[1]) was born 17 June 1846 in Fitchburg, Massachusetts, and died 08 January 1885 in Whitehall, Wisconsin. He married **Rheuamy Tucker** 14 February 1871 in Winooski, Wisconsin. She was born 13 October 1853 in Mitchell, Sheboygan County, Wisconsin.

Children of Otis Allen and Rheuamy Tucker are:

+	1275	i. William Otis[9] Allen, born 28 April 1872 in Winooski, Sheboygan County, Wisconsin.
	1276	ii. Kate Rheuamy Allen, born 20 February 1874 in Lincoln, Trempeleau County, Wisconsin.
	1277	iii. Vera Sarah Allen, born 24 July 1878 in Whitehall, Wisconsin.

1123. Ann Louisa[8] Blodgett (Louisa[7] Allen, Asenath[6] Colman, Susannah[5] Martin, John[4], Hannah[3] Darling, Denice[2], George[1]) was born 01 November 1828 in Boston, Massachusetts, and died 16 April 1895. She married **Samuel Stanton** 01 May 1851. He was born 01 October 1819 in Barnstead, New Hampshire, and died 14 February 1895.

Children of Ann Blodgett and Samuel Stanton are:

+	1278	i. Louis Chalmers[9] Stanton, born 25 April 1852 in Boston, Massachusetts.
	1279	ii. Ellen Louise Stanton, born 17 August 1853 in Newton, Massachusetts She married Herbert U. Weilbrecht 01 November 1876; born in London, England[1]
	1280	iii. Samuel Cecil Stanton, born 28 June 1855 in Newton, Massachusetts.

1164. Flora C.[8] Crooker (Eleanor[7] Darling, Zelek[6], Zeleck[5], William[4], Daniel[3], Denice[2], George[1]) was born 10 October 1845. She married **Edward Everett Cook**, son of Ira Cook and Julia Wilcox. He was born 20 September 1845 in Mendon, Massachusetts.

Children of Flora Crooker and Edward Cook are:

	1281	i. Olive[9] Cook, born 25 March 1806. She married Millins Taft
	1282	ii. Eliza Cook, born 25 March 1806; died June 1841.

1165. Caroline Lord Salisbury[8] Brown (Sarah[7] Salisbury, Rowena[6] Wheelock, Paul[5], Deborah[4] Darling, Benjamin[3], Denice[2], George[1]). She married **Lewis Curtis**.

Child of Caroline Brown and Lewis Curtis is:

1283   i.   Ellen[9] Curtis, born in Sheboggan, Wisconsin.

1172. Lydia Ann[8] Smith (Lydia[7] Salisbury, Rowena[6] Wheelock, Paul[5], Deborah[4] Darling, Benjamin[3], Denice[2], George[1]) was born 20 January 1815 in Adams, New York, and died 26 March 1858. She married **Peter Halmer Turner** 26 December 1836.

Children of Lydia Smith and Peter Turner are:
+ 1284   i.   Clarinda G.[9] Turner, born 24 January 1839 in Ellisburg, New York; died 24 April 1915 in Chicago, Illinois.
   1285   ii.   Chauncey Turner, born 07 September 1840; died August 1847.
   1286   iii. Sarah Turner, born 26 February 1843; died February 1927. She married Chandler P. Chapman 11 September 1866.
   1287   iv.   Mary Turner, born 07 December 1845 She married Elmer C. Dicey 07 December 1869.
   1288   v.   Ella Turner, born 17 September 1848. She married Jud C. Pierce 10 January 1873.
   1289   vi.   Francis Helmer Turner, born 19 September 1850 He married Mary Almy 30 July 1875.
   1290   vii. Kate Turner, born 01 September 1852. She married Elliott Holmes 1877.
   1291   viii. Jesse Smith Turner, born 20 July 1857. He married Florence Robinson 18 July 1892.

1176. Allen[8] Salisbury (Seneca Sales[7], Rowena[6] Wheelock, Paul[5], Deborah[4] Darling, Benjamin[3], Denice[2], George[1]) was born 23 December 1832 in Woodstock, Ohio, and died 23 February 1884 in Fairmount, Nebraska. He married **Mary Roberts.** She was born 05 October 1836 in near the foot of Mt. Snowdon in North Wales, 12 miles from Carnavron, and died 27 February 1924 in Aberdeen, South Dakota.

Child of Allen Salisbury and Mary Roberts is:
   1292   i.   Seneca Morris[9] Salisbury.

1181. Albert[8] Darling (Esseck[7], Darius[6], Ebenezer[5], Ebenezer[4], Benjamin[3], Denice[2], George[1]) was born 01 April 1843 in Burrillville, Rhode Island, and died 27 March 1928 in Connecticut. He married **(1) Mary Elizabeth Richards**. She was born 1843. He married **(2) Emma Webber** 24 March 1890. She was born 1855. He married **(3) Ellen Gildard** 09 August 1912.

Children of Albert Darling and Mary Richards are:

1293	i.	Emma Jane[9] Darling, born 03 September 1865.
1294	ii.	Newton Henry Darling, born July 1871.
1295	iii.	William Albert Darling, born 1876.
1296	iv.	George Washington Darling, born 1877.
1297	v.	Jesse Darling, born 21 August 1882.

1182. Ursula[8] Darling (Esseck[7], Darius[6], Ebenezer[5], Ebenezer[4], Benjamin[3], Denice[2], George[1]) was born July 1841 in Burrillville, Rhode Island, and died 1927 in Burrillville, Rhode Island.

Child of Ursula Darling is:

+	1298	i.	Charles H.[9] Darling, born 03 January 1859 in Burrillville, Rhode Island.

1206. Sumner[9] **Thayer** (Labin[8], Hannah[7] Taft, Nahum[6], Priscilla[5] Thayer, Ruth[4] Darling, Captain John[3], Denice[2], George[1]) was born November 1822 He married **Harriet Thayer** 01 November 1846.

Children of Sumner Thayer and Harriet Thayer are:

1299	i.	Frederick A. Thayer, born 26 October 1847 in Blackstone, Massachusetts.
1300	ii.	Frank Samuel Thayer, born 26 March 1850 in Blackstone, Massachusetts.
1301	iii.	Louisa A. Thayer, born 24 August 1852 in Blackstone, Massachusetts.
1302	iv.	Allie S. Thayer, born 28 November 1854 in Blackstone, Massachusetts.
1303	v.	Alfred Clayton Thayer, born 27 November 1856 in Blackstone, Massachusetts.
1304	vi.	Ezra Foster Thayer, born 09 July 1859 in Blackstone, Massachusetts.
1305	vii.	Ida May Thayer, born 07 September 1861 in Blackstone, Massachusetts.
1306	viii.	Anna W. Thayer, born 04 February 1864 in Blackstone, Massachusetts.
1307	ix.	Ernest Ebenezer Thayer, born 20 April 1866 in Blackstone, Massachusetts.

1214. Edwin Lambert[9] **Thayer** (Artemus[8], Hannah[7] Taft, Nahum[6], Priscilla[5] Thayer, Ruth[4] Darling, Captain John[3], Denice[2], George[1]) was born 03 November 1840. He married **Carrie Bliss** 10 September 1865.

Child of Edwin Thayer and Carrie Bliss is:

1308	i.	Lillian Alice Thayer, born 05 August 1867 in Woonsocket, Rhode Island.

1215. George H.[9] **Thayer** (Artemus[8], Hannah[7] Taft, Nahum[6], Priscilla[5] Thayer, Ruth[4] Darling, Captain John[3], Denice[2], George[1]) was born 10 October 1844. He married **Lucy B. Hadley** 14 June 1867.

Child of George Thayer and Lucy Hadley is:

    1309   i.   William H.[10] Thayer, born 27 March 1868 in Woonsocket, Rhode Island.

1242. Ira C.[9] **Darling** (Lucius[8], Samuel[7], Samuel[6], Samuel[5], Samuel[4], Captain John[3], Denice[2], George[1]) was born 1856, and died 21 July 1891 in Pawtucket, Rhode Island. He married **Louise McCloy**.

Children of Ira Darling and Louise McCloy are:

    1310   i.   Bessie E. Darling.
    1311   ii.   Carrie L. Darling.
    1312   iii.   Ira C. Darling. He married Agatha Louise Birkoff

1244. Ada E.[9] **Darling** (Lucius[8], Samuel[7], Samuel[6], Samuel[5], Samuel[4], Captain John[3], Denice[2], George[1]). She married **George Carpenter**.

Children of Ada Darling and George Carpenter are:

    1313   i.   Fanny D. Carpenter
    1314   ii.   Jennie D. Carpenter.

1266. Emily Lizzie[9] **Allen** (George Franklin[8], Henry[7], Asenath[6] Colman, Susannah[5] Martin, John[4], Hannah[3] Darling, Denice[2], George[1]) was born 24 September 1850 in Keene, New Hampshire. She married **Peter Frye** 10 November 1872 in Chatfield, Minnesota. He was born 16 October 1832 in Albany, Maine.

Child of Emily Allen and Peter Frye is:

    1315   i.   Arthur James Frye, born 20 June 1875 in Sparta, Wisconsin.

1271. Harry James^9 Allen (George Franklin^8, Henry^7, Asenath^6 Colman, Susannah^5 Martin, John^4, Hannah^3 Darling, Denice^2, George^1) was born 04 January 1869 in Chatfield, Minnesota. He married **Gertrude Alice Leach** 10 March 1891.

Child of Harry Allen and Gertrude Leach is:

    1316   i.   Gladys Gertrude^{10} Allen, born 27 February 1892 in Pleasent Grove, Minnesota.

1275. William Otis^9 Allen (Otis Jewett^8, Henry^7, Asenath^6 Colman, Susannah^5 Martin, John^4, Hannah^3 Darling, Denice^2, George^1) was born 28 April 1872 in Winooski, Sheboygan County, Wisconsin. He married **Annette Jane Bowen** 04 July 1893 in Marshfield, Wisconsin. She was born in Colby, Wisconsin.

Child of William Allen and Annette Bowen is:

    1317   i.   Lisle Forest^{10} Allen, born 26 November 1894 in Marshfield, Wisconsin.

1278. Louis Chalmers^9 Stanton (Ann Louisa^8 Blodgett, Louisa^7 Allen, Asenath^6 Colman, Susannah^5 Martin, John^4, Hannah^3 Darling, Denice^2, George^1) was born 25 April 1852 in Boston, Massachusetts. He married **Sarah Emma Bacon** 06 July 1882. She was born 16 April 1854 in Newton, Massachusetts.

Children of Louis Stanton and Sarah Bacon are:

    1318   i.   Harold Bacon^{10} Stanton, born 10 July 1883 in Newton, Massachusetts.

    1319   ii.   Bertha Stanton, born 28 October 1885 in Newton, Massachusetts

    1320   iii.   Malcolm Stanton, born 09 February 1888 in Newton, Massachusetts.

1284. Clarinda G.^{9} Turner (Lydia Ann^8 Smith, Lydia^7 Salisbury, Rowena^6 Wheelock, Paul^5, Deborah^4 Darling,

Benjamin[3], Denice[2], George[1]) was born 24 January 1839 in Ellisburg, New York, and died 24 April 1915 in Chicago, Illinois . She married **Elisha William Skinner,** 08 December 1858 in Palmyra, Wisconsin, son of Jacob Skinner and Polly Winters. He was born 08 September 1834 in Lanesboro, Pennsylvania.

Children of Clarinda Turner and Elisha Skinner are:

+   1321   i.   Jessie Gertrude[10] Skinner, born 25 February 1861 in Madison, Wisconsin; died 01 April 1923 in Chicago, Illinois.

     1322   ii.   Dwight Helmer Skinner, born 12 July 1863   He married Catherine Bingham

     1323   iii.   Allen Winters Skinner, born 06 October 1865   He married Minnie 03 July 1925.

     1324   iv.   Willey Skinner, born 06 October 1865; died in YOUNG.

     1325   v.   Frances Skinner, born 19 December 1876   She married Watson Ervine.

1298. Charles H.[9] Darling (Ursula[8], Esseck[7], Darius[6], Ebenezer[5], Ebenezer[4], Benjamin[3], Denice[2], George[1]) was born 03 January 1859 in Burrillville, Rhode Island. He married **(1) Mary Ann.** She was born 1858. He married **(2) Grace Cutler** 23 June 1896. She was born 1862.

Children of Charles Darling and Mary Ann are:

     1326   i.   Henry[10] Darling, born 25 January 1882.

     1327   ii.   Allen Darling, born 17 January 1886.

Generation No. 9

1321. Jessie Gertrude[10] Skinner (Clarinda G.[9] Turner, Lydia Ann[8] Smith, Lydia[7] Salisbury, Rowena[6] Wheelock, Paul[5], Deborah[4] Darling, Benjamin[3], Denice[2], George[1]) was born 25 February 1861 in Madison, Wisconsin, and died 01 April 1923 in Chicago, Illinois. She married **William de Garmo Turner** 16 October 1888 in Sioux City, Iowa, son of John Turner and Mary

Ellis. He was born 24 June 1865 in Jackson, California, and died 24 May 1915 in Chicago, Illinois.

Children of Jessie Skinner and William Turner are:

1328	i.	William deGarmo[11] Turner born 25 September 1889 in Sioux City, Iowa.
1329	ii.	Elisha Skinner Turner, born 19 July 1891 in Sioux City, Iowa.
1330	iii.	John Wallace Turner, born 10 June 1893 in Sioux City, Iowa.
1331	iv.	Olive Trowbridge Turner born 21 August 1895 in Sioux City, Iowa. She married John Wood MacArthur 05 June 1918; born 02 September 1889 in Buffalo, New York.
1332	v.	Helen Salisbury Turner, born 27 August 1897 in Evanston, Illinois
1333	vi.	Clarence Helmer Turner, born 24 December 1924.

INDEX

Alverson, Mercy, 61
Alverson, Uriah, 62
Amey, 59
Amidon, Hannah, 22
Amidon, Philip, 22
Anderson, Laura., 64
Angell, Mary, 92
Applin, Sarah, 11
Armington, Angeline, 121
Arnold, Harriet, 79
Arnold, Nathan, 37
Arnold, Patience, 114
Arnold, Richard, 46

B

Bacon, Sarah Emma, 130
Bacon, Susanna, 18
Baggs, Noble, 24
Baker, Joseph, 55
Balcom, Deborah, 27
Ballou, Abigail, 118
Ballou, Dennis, 96
Ballou, Duty, 60
Ballou, Flavius Josephus, 75
Ballou, Henry L., 103
Ballou, Joseph, 56
Ballou, Julia Ann, 96
Ballou, Levi, 76
Ballou, Martha, 75
Ballou, Mary, 43
Ballou, Nathan, 54
Ballou, Otis D., 78
Ballou, Rufus, 96
Ballou, Rufus Willis, 96
Ballou, Sarah, 39
Ballou, Uranah, 60
Ballou, Vienna, 76
Ballou/Wilcox, Mary, 80
Balmforth, Emma, 114
Barber, Elial, 97

Barney, Martha, 66
Barney, Sarah, 92
Barney, Thomas, 66
Barton, Mary, 72
Bates, J.R., 112
Battles, Deborah, 64
Battles, Edward, 26
Battles, Hannah, 26
Battles, Jeremiah, 26
Battles, Susanna, 26
Beach, George, 55
Beach, Ruth Ann, 89
Beckett, Mary, 8
Bennett, Deborah, 67
Bennett, Hannah, 67
Bennett, John, 67
Bennett, Joseph, 67
Bennett, Levinah, 67
Bennett, Olive, 67
Bennett, Susanna, 67
Bennett, Timothy, 67
Benson, Abigail, 62
Benson, Benoni, 6
Benson, Job, 18
Benson, John, 32
Benson, Samuel, 32
Benson, Sarah, 18
Benson, Susanna, 6, 53
Billings, Anna, 24
Bingham, Catherine, 131
Birkoff, Agatha Louise, 129
Blake, Elias, 94, 95
Blake, Huldah, 27
Blake, Jeremiah Darling, 95
Blake, Nancy, 94
Blake, Samuel, 95
Blake, Sarah, 49
Blake, Susannah, 9
Bliss, Carrie, 128
Blodgett, Ann Louisa, 107, 125

Blodgett, Benjamin Colman, 107
Blodgett, Frances Amelia, 108
Blodgett, Henry, 107
Blodgett, William Henry, 108
Bosworth, Elizabeth, 14
Bosworth, Eunice, 15
Bosworth, Henry, 3, 14
Bosworth, Ichabod, 14
Bosworth, Mary, 14
Bosworth, Mary R., 122
Bosworth, Rachel, 15
Bowditch, Matilda, 68
Bowen, Annette Jane, 130
Bowen, Candace, 58
Bowen, Clarissa, 113
Bowen, Cyrel, 113
Bowen, Eleazer, 57, 58
Bowen, Fidelia, 113
Bowen, Harris, 113
Bowen, James, 58
Bowen, Lydia, 57
Bowen, Martin, 58
Bowen, Rhoda, 58
Bowman, Charlotte, 20
Boyce, Benjamin, 18
Boyce, Daniel, 18
Boyden, John R., 103
Bradish, Emeline L., 123
Brown, Abigail, 15
Brown, Anna, 15
Brown, Caleb, 12
Brown, Caroline Lord Salisbury, 125
Brown, Gideon, 15, 42
Brown, Haley, 111
Brown, Hannah, 42
Brown, Ichabod, 15, 30, 41
Brown, John, 12, 15
Brown, Joseph, 12
Brown, Joshua, 12

Brown, Levi, 12
Brown, Lydia, 15, 30
Brown, Martha, 15
Brown, Peter, 15
Brown, Samuel, 15, 30
Brown, William, 12
Bruce, Martha, 66
Bullard, Judith, 52
Burdish, Phebe, 91
Burr, Sarah, 75
Burroughs, Eleanor, 65
Butler, Cyrus, 87
Butman, John, 61
Butterworth, Penelope, 12
Buxton, Samuel, 11

C

Cady, Atwood, 48
Capron, Elisha, 76
Capron, Joseph, 37
Carpenter, Adeline, 112
Carpenter, Charles, 53
Carpenter, Fanny D, 129
Carpenter, George, 129
Carpenter, Jennie D., 129
Carrary, Stephen, 36
Carrell, Benjamin, 29
Carrell, James, 29
Carrell, Jared, 29
Carrell, Joseph, 29
Carter, Eliza S., 84
Carter, Margaret, 84
Cass, Jarvis, 105
Chapin, Charles, 100
Chapin, Cyrus, 101
Chapin, Elias, 100
Chapin, Hollis, 101
Chapin, Joseph, 35
Chapin, Maria, 100
Chapman, Chandler P., 126

Cheney, Caleb, 22
Cheney, Sarah, 27
Chickering, Nathaniel, 14
Chilson, Diadama Cook, 120
Chilson, Eliza Ellen, 120
Chilson, James Olney, 120
Chilson, John, 39
Chilson, Lewis Morton, 120
Chilson, Libbeus, 120
Chilson, Margaretta, 105
Chilson, Mariana, 120
Chilson, Martha Whipple, 120
Chilson, Mary E., 120
Chilson, Orrin, 120
Chilson, Reuben, 120
Chison, John, 119
Chison, John Draper, 120
Chison, Lucius Addison, 120
Church, George M., 87
Church, Hannah, 80
Church, Henry Augustus, 87
Church, Joseph, 86
Church, Mary Elizabeth, 87
Church, Peter, 86
Church, Sarah, 87
Church, William Marshall, 87
Claflin, John, 21
Clark, Annie, 115
Clark, Archibald, 73
Clark, Eddy, 80
Clark, Experience, 21
Clark, Jepthah, 28
Clark, Rachel, 80, 99, 104
Clark, Susanna, 40
Clark, William A., 105
Clayton, Alfred, 128
Clemons, Martha P., 74
Cobb, John, 69
Cobb, Mary/Polly, 69
Coe, Hiram, 47

Colburn, Levi P., 102
Colby, Dorothy, 20
Cole, James, 94
Cole, Lydia, 94
Collins, Martha, 124
Colman, Asenath, 44, 81
Colman, Benjamin, 44
Comstock, Lucina, 61
Comstock, Nathan, 61
Constantine, Jacob, 106
Constantine, Sally, 106
Constock, Ann, 61
Cook, Aaron, 99
Cook, Aaron Clark, 105
Cook, Albertus, 79
Cook, Alfred, 60
Cook, Almira, 100, 119
Cook, Almira B., 103, 118
Cook, Alpha, 77, 100
Cook, Amos, 78
Cook, Ann Eliza, 119
Cook, Ann Janetta, 103
Cook, Ann Olivia, 103
Cook, Anne, 25
Cook, Anson, 104
Cook, Anson Eddy, 105
Cook, Arnold, 78
Cook, Barton, 79
Cook, Betsey, 61
Cook, Celina, 37
Cook, Charles M., 61
Cook, Cyrene J., 103
Cook, Daniel, 25
Cook, Davis, 78, 118
Cook, Diadema, 100, 120
Cook, Eddy Clark, 105
Cook, Edmund L., 79
Cook, Edna L., 103
Cook, Edward Everett, 125
Cook, Edward Lyman, 104
Cook, Elbridge Gerry, 61

Cook, Elias, 99, 118
Cook, Elias S., 118
Cook, Eliphalet, 103
Cook, Eliza, 78, 125
Cook, Elizabeth Jillson, 105
Cook, Ellen M., 119
Cook, Ellis, 78
Cook, Esek, 98
Cook, Fenner, 100
Cook, Francis, 97
Cook, George Smith, 104
Cook, Gertrude, 103
Cook, Hannah J., 120
Cook, Henry Lyman, 104
Cook, Horace C., 103
Cook, James, 75, 99
Cook, James Madison, 77
Cook, Jennie, 119
Cook, Joanna, 75
Cook, Lavina, 99
Cook, Lavinia, 94
Cook, Levi, 77
Cook, Levi Lee, 79
Cook, Levice, 39
Cook, Louisa A., 61
Cook, Lucie E., 99
Cook, Lucina S., 119
Cook, Lucinda, 54
Cook, Lucius Olney, 99
Cook, Lucy, 25, 61
Cook, Lydia, 5
Cook, Lyman Arnold, 77, 99, 103, 118
Cook, Margery, 43, 46
Cook, Maria, 61
Cook, Mary Ann W., 100
Cook, Mary Maria, 105
Cook, Maxcy, 61
Cook, Medora, 103
Cook, Michael, 75
Cook, Milton, 61

Cook, Miranda, 60, 75, 99
Cook, Nancy, 37
Cook, Naomi, 36
Cook, Nathan Aldrich, 99
Cook, Nathaniel, 60, 75, 86
Cook, Olive, 79, 99, 125
Cook, Olney, 75
Cook, Olney M., 79
Cook, Onley, 75
Cook, Perley, 77
Cook, Phebe, 75, 104
Cook, Phila, 75
Cook, Priscilla, 24, 89
Cook, Rachel, 105
Cook, Reuben, 75, 99
Cook, Reuben Olney, 100
Cook, Sally, 77, 79, 98
Cook, Samantha B., 119
Cook, Samuel, 5
Cook, Selina, 75
Cook, Sena Ann, 99
Cook, Seviah, 40
Cook, Silas, 37, 74, 75, 99
Cook, Stephen, 99
Cook, Stillman R., 99
Cook, Susan A., 103
Cook, Susan Ann, 105
Cook, Susanna, 40
Cook, Vienna, 60
Cook, Walter, 43
Cook, Whipple, 37, 60, 61
Cook, Willis, 77, 103
Cook, Winslow, 60
Cook, Ziba, 75, 98
Cooper, Mary, 98
Corbett, Joseph, 43
Corbett, Margery, 43
Corbett, Mehitable, 43
Cox, Permilla, 51
Crandall, Reuben G., 103
Crooker, Flora C., 111, 125

Crooker, William, 111
Crooks, Deborah, 81
Crooks, Jeremiah, 81
Crooks, Joel, 81
Crooks, Phebe, 81
Crooks, Polly, 81
Crooks, Sally, 81
Crosett, Polly, 54
Crossman, Samuel, 21
Curtis, Ellen, 126
Curtis, Lewis, 125
Curtis, Thaddeus, 77
Cutler, Grace, 131
Cutler, Sarah, 55

D

Danforth, Sarah, 81
Daniels, Ephraim, 6
Darling, 89
Darling, Aaron, 1, 20, 23, 50
Darling, Abel, 31, 69
Darling, Abigail, 2, 3, 5, 7, 8, 9, 13, 14, 17, 19, 21, 26, 32, 34, 39, 41
Darling, Abisha, 40
Darling, Abner, 5, 18
Darling, Ada E., 121, 129
Darling, Adeline, 87
Darling, Ahimaaz, 40, 80
Darling, Ahimaz, 80, 105
Darling, Albert, 92, 94, 113, 127
Darling, Alden, 43, 80, 81
Darling, Allen, 131
Darling, Allister, 71
Darling, Almon, 59
Darling, Alpheus, 29, 65
Darling, Alston, 92
Darling, Alva, 50
Darling, Alvin, 59

Darling, Amasa, 41
Darling, Amey, 17, 58, 113
Darling, Amos, 97, 116
Darling, Andrew, 24, 56, 57, 90, 91
Darling, Angell, 92, 114
Darling, Anna, 3, 8, 15, 25, 29, 30, 40, 58, 93
Darling, Anna Sarah, 92
Darling, Anne Frances, 114
Darling, Anson, 59
Darling, Artemus, 47, 48, 84
Darling, Artemus Amasa, 85
Darling, Asa, 76, 100
Darling, Barton, 59, 93
Darling, Bathsheba, 34, 72
Darling, Benjamin, 2, 6, 7, 23, 25, 29, 37, 59
Darling, Benjamin Young, 65
Darling, Benson, 19, 48
Darling, Bessie E., 129
Darling, Bethany, 46
Darling, Byron, 121
Darling, Caleb, 27, 47, 62
Darling, Calvin, 68, 70
Darling, Captain John, 1
Darling, Caroline, 76
Darling, Caroline Idelia, 84, 85
Darling, Carrie B., 115
Darling, Carrie L., 129
Darling, Charles, 64, 84, 94, 101
Darling, Charles H., 127, 131
Darling, Charles Wheeler, 87
Darling, Charles White, 65, 94
Darling, Charlotte, 55
Darling, Charlotte Amanda, 96
Darling, Chloe, 53, 61, 63

Darling, Christina, 21
Darling, Collins, 76
Darling, Cornelius, 1
Darling, Cornelius, 1, 4, 16, 43
Darling, Cortez, 65
Darling, Cyrus, 49, 87
Darling, Daniel, 1, 5, 18, 46, 68
Darling, Daniel Franklin, 70
Darling, Darius, 25, 47, 57, 59, 91
Darling, David, 4, 15, 19, 24, 31, 47, 48, 56, 67, 68, 90
Darling, David Allen, 90
Darling, David Sanford, 95
Darling, Deborah, 3, 7, 14, 22, 24, 27, 29, 30, 43, 49
Darling, Denice, 1
Darling, Dennis Albert, 93
Darling, Dinnis, 27
Darling, Dora, 116
Darling, Dorcas, 24, 55, 57
Darling, Ebenezer, 1, 3, 7, 9, 17, 24, 34, 57
Darling, Edmond, 92
Darling, Edmund Adams, 121
Darling, Edward, 64
Darling, Edward Everett, 85
Darling, Edwin, 101, 102, 121, 122
Darling, Edwin Crawford, 88
Darling, Ehud, 20, 50
Darling, Elathan, 45
Darling, Eleanor, 88, 111
Darling, Eli, 51, 95
Darling, Elias, 31, 68
Darling, Elihue, 58
Darling, Elijah, 16, 24, 25, 42, 55, 68
Darling, Elisha, 47, 83, 115
Darling, Eliza, 60, 115

Darling, Elizabeth, 1, 2, 3, 5, 7, 8, 9, 12, 13, 16, 24, 27, 30, 31, 32, 38, 43, 50, 81, 90, 93
Darling, Elizabeth R., 84
Darling, Ellen Maria, 115
Darling, Elmira, 51
Darling, Emily, 77
Darling, Emma Jane, 95, 127
Darling, Enoch, 15, 23, 42, 54, 81
Darling, Ephraim, 23
Darling, Erwin, 92
Darling, Esek, 97, 116
Darling, Esseck, 91, 113
Darling, Estes, 87
Darling, Esther, 10, 31, 37, 68, 76
Darling, Etta, 116
Darling, Eunice, 31, 55, 61, 95
Darling, Fanny, 68
Darling, Fidelia, 92
Darling, Floyd Everett, 108
Darling, Francis, 115
Darling, Freelove, 51
Darling, Fuller, 50
Darling, Gardner, 51
Darling, George, 63, 65, 83, 89, 90, 91, 97, 101, 115
Darling, George Barney, 94
Darling, George Henry, 122
Darling, George Samuel, 96
Darling, George Seth, 84
Darling, George Washington, 127
Darling, Geroge Curtis, 122
Darling, Gideon, 67
Darling, Gilbert, 101
Darling, Grace, 122
Darling, Hannah, 1, 2, 3, 5, 7, 8, 13, 26, 31, 32, 40, 47, 67, 70, 96

Darling, Harriet, 68, 84, 95
Darling, Harrison, 50
Darling, Helam, 70
Darling, Henry, 27, 61, 62, 84, 91, 93, 103, 108, 127, 131
Darling, Hopey, 56
Darling, Horace, 50, 63, 91
Darling, Horatio Nelson, 50
Darling, Huldah, 16, 47
Darling, Ichabod, 53
Darling, Ida Elizabeth, 121
Darling, Idelia Taft, 85
Darling, Ira C., 121, 129
Darling, Irene, 55
Darling, Irving Taft, 109
Darling, Isaac, 50, 83, 90
Darling, Isabella, 93
Darling, Jacob, 24, 55, 67, 83
Darling, James, 23, 31, 38, 45, 67, 68, 91, 94
Darling, James Benson, 84
Darling, James C., 55, 90
Darling, James Edmond, 84, 108
Darling, James G., 92
Darling, Jane, 4, 17
Darling, Jane Frances, 51
Darling, Jason, 63
Darling, Jefferson, 64
Darling, Jefferson Burr, 76, 101
Darling, Jemima, 31, 34
Darling, Jerusha, 13, 31, 37, 53, 58, 89
Darling, Jesse, 18, 45, 95, 127
Darling, Joab, 34
Darling, Joanna, 28, 37, 62, 65, 74
Darling, Joannah, 25
Darling, Job, 16, 19, 43, 46

Darling, John, 2, 4, 8, 9, 10, 13, 23, 24, 29, 30, 31, 32, 38, 39, 41, 43, 49, 51, 64, 66, 67, 71, 81, 96
Darling, John Adams, 77, 102
Darling, John Kimton, 71
Darling, John L., 116
Darling, John Metcalf, 68
Darling, John Oliver, 122
Darling, John Quincy, 97
Darling, John Quincy Adams, 103
Darling, John Russell, 55
Darling, Jonathan, 23
Darling, Joseph, 7, 10, 23, 34, 53
Darling, Josephine, 96
Darling, Joshua, 13, 32, 40, 47, 67, 70
Darling, Joshua Barney, 70
Darling, Judson, 50
Darling, Julia, 122
Darling, Kezia, 5, 20, 53
Darling, Labiron, 70
Darling, Lanson, 76
Darling, Lavina, 20
Darling, Leah, 19
Darling, Leonard, 64
Darling, Levi, 20, 49, 53
Darling, Levi Lincoln, 93
Darling, Levory, 70
Darling, Lewis, 62, 64, 70
Darling, Limon, 62
Darling, Lloyd, 122
Darling, Lois, 69
Darling, Lorainia, 67
Darling, Louisa, 51
Darling, Lovinia, 121
Darling, Luann, 87
Darling, Lucinia, 95
Darling, Lucius, 101, 121

Darling, Lucius Bowles, 121
Darling, Lucretia, 56
Darling, Lucy, 27, 34, 37, 53, 60
Darling, Luke, 25, 54
Darling, Lyddia, 70
Darling, Lydia, 5, 16, 18, 21, 23, 42, 50, 54, 56, 57, 61, 68, 90, 94
Darling, Lyman, 48, 83
Darling, Lyman Augustus, 84
Darling, Lyman Morse, 101
Darling, Mabel, 122
Darling, Mabel Bowen, 109
Darling, Madison, 64
Darling, Marcia, 51
Darling, Margaret, 3, 8, 10
Darling, Margery, 89, 112
Darling, Margus, 71
Darling, Maria, 70, 83, 108, 115
Darling, Marshall, 95
Darling, Martha, 3, 11, 24, 31, 50, 58, 66, 83
Darling, Martha Salone, 113
Darling, Mary, 2, 3, 4, 8, 10, 14, 16, 18, 20, 24, 30, 31, 32, 38, 39, 41, 43, 46, 47, 56, 57, 69, 93, 95
Darling, Mary Ann, 51, 90, 93, 102
Darling, Mary Elizabeth, 103, 122
Darling, Mary Evelyn, 121
Darling, Mary Jane, 90
Darling, Mary Sophia, 85
Darling, Mary Young, 94
Darling, Mary/Polly, 68
Darling, Matthew, 18, 45
Darling, Mattie, 109
Darling, Mayo Cook, 102

Darling, Mehitable, 7, 27
Darling, Melancy Lawton, 88
Darling, Melissa, 90
Darling, Mercy, 34, 48
Darling, Michael, 13, 38, 41
Darling, Milla, 37
Darling, Minnie E., 115
Darling, Molly, 68
Darling, Moses, 23, 61
Darling, Moses Leland, 50
Darling, Moses Oscar, 85, 108
Darling, Nabby, 91
Darling, Nancy, 55, 59, 68, 69, 76, 94
Darling, Nancy Ann, 84
Darling, Nancy Jane, 85
Darling, Nathan, 29, 37, 58, 64, 69, 95
Darling, Nathaniel, 40, 65
Darling, Nelson, 91, 113
Darling, Nelson Strong, 93
Darling, Newbury, 70
Darling, Newton, 59, 69, 95
Darling, Olive, 37, 46, 78
Darling, Oliver, 34, 90
Darling, Ora Weston, 114
Darling, Oscar, 122
Darling, Oscar Eugene, 109
Darling, Otis, 71
Darling, Palmer, 50
Darling, Pamelia, 66
Darling, Pardon, 2
Darling, Patty, 41
Darling, Pelatiah, 8, 31, 32, 38, 69
Darling, Penelope, 9, 13, 39, 41
Darling, Permilla, 51
Darling, Peter, 5, 7, 24, 25, 27, 31, 34, 49, 58, 61, 89

Darling, Phebe, 16, 34, 43, 46, 81
Darling, Phila, 40, 70
Darling, Philander, 51
Darling, Phineas, 32, 71
Darling, Phoebe, 90
Darling, Polly, 55, 70, 90
Darling, Precilla, 58
Darling, Prudence, 28, 39, 51, 54, 63
Darling, Rachel, 3, 9, 10, 13, 16, 19, 21, 24, 28, 32, 42, 61, 62
Darling, Ransom, 50
Darling, Rebecca, 50, 91
Darling, Reuben, 26, 37, 60
Darling, Rhoda, 28, 37, 76, 77, 100
Darling, Richard, 4, 17, 25, 81
Darling, Riley, 92, 114
Darling, Robert Gould, 122
Darling, Rodney Luther, 88
Darling, Rowena, 93
Darling, Roxanna, 50
Darling, Rozellany, 70
Darling, Ruel, 101
Darling, Rufus, 70, 93, 96
Darling, Ruhamah, 15, 16
Darling, Ruth, 2, 3, 8, 9, 11, 13, 25, 32, 34, 38, 47, 50, 72, 83, 90
Darling, Sabra, 34, 37
Darling, Sadie B., 115
Darling, Sally, 61
Darling, Samatha, 95
Darling, Samuel, 2, 3, 5, 7, 9, 12, 13, 18, 27, 31, 33, 36, 37, 41, 48, 69, 75, 76, 95, 101, 121
Darling, Sarah, 1, 3, 4, 19, 38, 40, 46, 55, 56, 62, 90

Darling, Sarah Ann, 51, 65, 92, 114
Darling, Sarah Augusta, 102
Darling, Sarah Burr, 76
Darling, Sarah Freeman, 77
Darling, Seth, 2, 29, 32, 40, 48, 63
Darling, Seth Benson, 85
Darling, Silencey, 56
Darling, Simeon, 29, 35, 49, 64, 72
Darling, Simon, 72, 94
Darling, Smith, 63
Darling, Smith Walling, 108
Darling, Socrates, 50
Darling, Solomon, 93
Darling, Stephen, 23, 25, 40, 48, 51, 53
Darling, Susan, 60, 64
Darling, Susan Alvina, 97
Darling, Susan H., 115
Darling, Susanna, 31
Darling, Susannah, 5, 19
Darling, Thankful, 56
Darling, Theodore, 116
Darling, Thomas, 7, 28, 56, 64, 93
Darling, Thomas Jefferson, 55, 89
Darling, Thomas West, 93
Darling, Timothy, 10, 16, 25, 34, 35, 42, 81
Darling, Trial, 20, 27
Darling, Urania, 48
Darling, Uriah, 40
Darling, Ursula, 113, 127
Darling, Vienna, 77
Darling, Walter Emerson, 121
Darling, Walter Eugene, 109
Darling, Warren, 48, 60
Darling, Welcome, 25, 26, 59

Holbrook, Rachel, 54, 63
Holbrook, Reuben, 62
Holbrook, Samuel, 54
Holbrook, Sarah, 36
Holbrook, Silvanus, 36
Holbrook, Stephen, 54
Holland, Thomas, 14
Holmes, Elliott, 126
How, Joseph, 7
Howe, Joseph, 27
Howell, William H., 87
Hubbard, Lucy Ann, 82
Hubbard, Sarah Caroline, 82
Hullock, Ovet, 110
Humes, Nicholas, 19
Humes, Samuel, 19
Hunt, Daniel, 20
Hunt, Elizabeth, 30, 65
Hunt, George, 20
Hunt, John, 20, 27, 30, 53
Hunt, Keziah, 20, 49, 53
Hunt, Mary, 18, 30
Hunt, Peter, 20
Hunt, Rhoda, 20
Hunt, Samuel, 30
Hunt, Sarah, 86
Hunt, Seth, 20
Hunter, Manley, 90
Huntley, Hannah, 33
Hurlbut, Jesse, 72

I

Ingerson, Frederick A., 119
Inman, Abigail, 26
Inman, Anna, 26
Inman, Bathsheba, 34
Inman, Clara Emma, 108
Inman, Edward, 26
Inman, Elisha, 26
Inman, Elizabeth, 26

Inman, Huldah, 72
Inman, Joseph, 34
Inman, Martha, 26
Inman, Mary, 26
Inman, Penelope, 26
Inman, Priscilla, 26
Inman, Rhoda, 72
Inman, Ruth, 113
Inman, Samuel, 26
Inman, Stephen, 72
Inman, Susannah, 26
Irons, Francis, 84

J

Jackson, Sarah, 14
Jefferds, John G., 121
Jencks, Rebecca Ellen, 116
Jenks, Ellen, 97
Jillson, Anna, 10, 39
Jillson, Ella Ann, 78
Jillson, Lavina, 59
Jillson, Marieta P., 92
Jillson, Nathan, 59, 92
Jillson, Uriah, 39
Jillson, Waitstill, 60
Jones, Catherine, 93
Jones, Daniel, 40
Jones, Elias, 31
Jones, Lorraine, 50

K

Keach, Freelove, 114
Keith, Gersham, 18
Keith, Henry, 23
Keith, Jean, 72
Kellogg, Lois, 65
Kendall, Nancy Smith, 82
Kimton, Bethia, 71
King, Sallie/Sarah, 112
Knapp, Ebenezer, 27

145

Knight, John, 31

L

Lamb, Estus, 52
Leach, Gertrude Alice, 130
Lee, George Barney, 94
Legg, John, 12
Leland, Abigail, 42
Leland, James, 42
Leland, Sylvia, 100
Leonard, Harriet, 95
Lewis, Harriet, 82
Lewis, Martin, 73
Lewis, Mary, 23
Lewis, Sarah M., 109
Lincoln, Samuel, 79
Livermore, Abel, 106
Livermore, Benjamin Wesley,
    106
Livermore, Burr, 106
Livermore, Eliza Janet, 106,
    123
Livermore, Elvira Wilson,
    106, 123
Livermore, Giles, 106
Livermore, Miles, 106
Livermore, William Adelbert,
    106
Lovering, Anna, 95
Luther, Edward Arnold, 85

M

MacArthur, John Wood, 132
Malowery, Mary, 26
Marble, John, 10
Marsh, Chloe, 63
Marsh, Joseph, 63
Marsh, Nancy, 63
Marshall, Sarah, 46
Martin, John, 5, 17

Martin, Julianne, 89
Martin, Lydia A., 100
Martin, Mary, 5
Martin, Susannah, 17
Martin, Susannah5, 44
Martin, Thomas, 5
Mason, Anna, 12, 15
Mason, Olney, 77
Mathewson, Albert, 56
Mathewson, Darling, 56
Matthews, Marenus, 112
McCaw, William, 123
McCloy, Louise, 129
McGrafth, Lydia, 84
McKee, Leonard, 63
Medbury, Benjamin, 27, 28
Medbury, Darling, 28
Medbury, David, 28
Medbury, Edward, 28
Medbury, Isaac, 28
Medbury, Joseph, 28
Medbury, Mary, 28
Medbury, Nathan, 28
Medbury, Nathaniel, 28
Medbury, Ruth, 28
Merriam, Timothy, 47
Merritt, Phebe, 80
Metcalf, Esther, 67
Metcalf, John, 68
Mitchell, John, 4
Mitchell, Mary, 66
Mitchell, Ruth, 98
Mitchell, Sarah, 4
Moody, Martha, 75
Moon, Abraham, 98
Moon, Mary, 98
Morse, Deborah, 29
Morse, Elizabeth, 2
Morse, Julia/Judith, 101
Morse, Samuel, 2
Mowry, Jacob, 8

Russell, Solomon, 93
Russell, Theodocia, 93

S

Salisbury, Abigail, 89
Salisbury, Allen, 112, 126
Salisbury, Daniel, 66
Salisbury, Deborah, 106
Salisbury, Edward, 88, 89
Salisbury, Lucy, 89
Salisbury, Lydia, 89, 111
Salisbury, Martha, 66
Salisbury, Nicholas, 88
Salisbury, Samuel, 66
Salisbury, Sarah, 89, 111
Salisbury, Seneca Morris, 126
Salisbury, Seneca Sales, 89, 112
Salisbury, Silas, 89
Salisbury, Thomas, 65
Saunders, Prussia, 65
Sayles, Lydia, 29, 52
Sayles, Nancy, 62
Sayles, Stephen, 76
Scott, Elizabeth, 53
Scott, Rebecca, 25
Scott, Samuel, 40
Sheffield, Thomasin, 12
Sheldon, Susannah, 59
Sheppard, Daniel, 19
Sherman, Patience, 75
Shippee, Mary, 113
Short, Nathaniel, 79
Simmon, John, 98
Simmon, Susan Mitchell, 98
Skinner, Allen Winters, 131
Skinner, Dwight Helmer, 131
Skinner, Elisha William, 131
Skinner, Frances, 131
Skinner, Jessie Gertrude, 131

Skinner, Willey, 131
Slack, Benjamin, 36
Slack, Esther, 27, 33, 36
Sleeman, Mary, 6
Slocum, Mary, 6
Smith, Adelibe DeMontall, 112
Smith, Caroline Lord, 112
Smith, Chauncey, 111, 112
Smith, Clarinda A., 112
Smith, David, 111
Smith, Deborah, 34
Smith, Jane Antoinette, 112
Smith, Joanna, 102
Smith, Lavina B., 104
Smith, Lydia Ann, 112, 126
Smith, Margaret, 101
Smith, Prudence, 28
Smith, Rhoda, 11
Smith, Rowena Wheelock, 111
Smith, Sarah Wawkins, 112
Smith, Ursula Hawley, 112
Smith, Willard, 112
Snell, Maria, 89
Snow, Franklin A., 122
Snow, Ivory, 54
Southwick, Hannah, 45
Southwick, Joseph, 19
Spofford, Hannah, 4
Sprague, Amanda, 114
Sprague, Anna, 114
Sprague, Bently, 110
Sprague, Caroline, 114
Sprague, Daniel, 42
Sprague, David Daniel, 109
Sprague, Elijah, 114
Sprague, Emerson, 110
Sprague, Enos M., 110
Sprague, Francis, 114
Sprague, Gallusha, 111

Sprague, George, 86, 110, 114
Sprague, Gideon, 86, 110
Sprague, Heman, 109
Sprague, Henry, 110
Sprague, Hiram, 111
Sprague, James, 57
Sprague, Jane, 110
Sprague, Jemima, 86
Sprague, John T., 109
Sprague, Joseph, 86, 109
Sprague, Julia, 110
Sprague, Levina, 110
Sprague, Lucinda, 111
Sprague, Malissa, 111
Sprague, Manassah, 86, 110
Sprague, Manasseh, 86
Sprague, Mary, 86, 110, 111
Sprague, Mary G., 110
Sprague, Mercy, 110
Sprague, Noble, 111
Sprague, Norman, 110
Sprague, Phineas, 86, 110
Sprague, Rebecca, 109
Sprague, Sarah, 110
Sprague, Sarah Jane, 111
Sprague, Sirena, 111
Sprague, Stephen M., 109
Sprague, Susannah, 111
Sprague, Sylvester, 110
Stacy, Sarah, 14
Stanton, Bertha, 130
Stanton, Ellen Louise, 125
Stanton, Harold Bacon, 130
Stanton, Louis Chalmers, 125, 130
Stanton, Malcolm, 130
Stanton, Samuel, 125
Stanton, Samuel Cecil, 125
Staples, Abraham, 8
Staples, Deborah, 63
Staples, Hannah, 8, 38, 41, 65

Staples, Lavina, 99
Staples, Martha Bartlett, 17
Staples, Mary, 25
Staples, Nabor, 28
Stearns, Lucy, 83
Stearns, Nathan, 84
Stearns, Susan, 84
Steele, Emily, 68
Steere, Sarah, 56
Stone, Theodocia, 68
Strong, Josiah, 86
Sumner, Jesse, 40
Sumner, Martha, 21
Sweet, Anna, 57
Sweet, Dorcas, 57
Sweet, Elizabeth, 57
Sweet, Esther, 57
Sweet, Henry, 110
Sweet, Jeremiah, 57
Sweet, Justin, 109
Sweet, Maria Amelia, 122
Sweet, Mary, 57
Sweet, Mary Ann, 109
Sweet, Oliver, 122
Sweet, Timothy, 57

T

Taft, Abner, 35, 73
Taft, Caleb, 36
Taft, Darius, 73
Taft, Diana, 36
Taft, Gideon, 110
Taft, Hannah, 73, 97
Taft, James, 35
Taft, Joanna, 35, 54
Taft, Joel, 35
Taft, Joseph, 33, 35, 36
Taft, Josiah, 36
Taft, Laura, 110
Taft, Lorinda, 47, 85

Taft, Luke, 35
Taft, Margaret, 35, 36
Taft, Mary, 35, 73, 97
Taft, Mary (Susan), 48
Taft, Mary Susan, 86
Taft, Mercy, 96
Taft, Millins, 125
Taft, Moses, 35, 36, 73
Taft, Nahum, 35, 73
Taft, Nathum, 36
Taft, Oliver, 73
Taft, Phila, 69
Taft, Phineas, 48
Taft, Polly, 72
Taft, Priscilla, 35, 36
Taft, Reuben, 33, 72
Taft, Rizpah, 113
Taft, Ruth, 35
Taft, Sally, 110
Taft, Samuel, 64
Taft, Sarah, 32
Taft, Susan, 108
Taft, Sylvia, 48
Taft, Timothy, 35, 36
Taft, Trial, 73
Taft, Webb, 73
Taylor, Ann, 112
Taylor, Elizabeth, 86
Taylor, George, 112
Taylor, Hannah, 112
Taylor, John, 112
Taylor, Sopia, 112
Thain, Thomas, 60
Thayer, Abigail, 8, 33, 73, 74, 116
Thayer, Adelaide, 116
Thayer, Albert H., 117
Thayer, Alexander, 52
Thayer, Allie S., 128
Thayer, Almira, 83
Thayer, Anna W., 128

Thayer, Ansley, 98
Thayer, Ariel, 117
Thayer, Artemus, 97, 117
Thayer, Asenath, 104
Thayer, Charlotte, 44
Thayer, Chloe, 73
Thayer, Clara E., 117
Thayer, Clarissa Adams, 116
Thayer, Clarissa E., 117
Thayer, Cyrene, 103
Thayer, Cyrene E., 117
Thayer, Cyrus, 83
Thayer, David, 72
Thayer, Dency, 52
Thayer, Ebenezer, 37, 53
Thayer, Edwin Lambert, 117, 128
Thayer, Elijah, 33
Thayer, Elizabeth, 9, 12, 33, 74, 83
Thayer, Elmer James, 117
Thayer, Emery, 74
Thayer, Ernest Ebenezer, 128
Thayer, Eunice, 74
Thayer, Experience, 10, 52
Thayer, Ezra Foster, 128
Thayer, Faithful, 72
Thayer, Ferdinando, 3
Thayer, Frank Samuel, 128
Thayer, Frederick A., 128
Thayer, George H., 117, 129
Thayer, George Henry, 117
Thayer, George Washington, 74, 98, 117
Thayer, Haddasha, 45
Thayer, Hannah, 36, 97
Thayer, Hannah Rebecca, 117
Thayer, Harriet, 128
Thayer, Henry, 74, 98
Thayer, Hezekiah, 4
Thayer, Huldah, 22, 29

Thayer, Hyram, 74
Thayer, Ida May, 128
Thayer, Isaac, 8, 14, 17
Thayer, Jacob, 45
Thayer, Jarvis, 44, 82, 83
Thayer, Jemima, 45
Thayer, Jerusha, 53
Thayer, Jesse, 18
Thayer, John, 8, 14, 17, 44
Thayer, John B., 83
Thayer, John H., 74, 83, 98
Thayer, Jonathan, 3
Thayer, Joseph, 104
Thayer, Jotham, 52
Thayer, Julia, 100
Thayer, Labin, 97, 116
Thayer, Lewis, 98
Thayer, Lillian Alice, 128
Thayer, Louisa A., 128
Thayer, Lucinda Ann, 98
Thayer, Lucretia, 52
Thayer, Lydia, 18
Thayer, Marvin, 98
Thayer, Mary, 44, 83, 98
Thayer, Mercy, 19
Thayer, Miranda, 97
Thayer, Moses, 103
Thayer, Nahum Pond, 82
Thayer, Nancy, 83
Thayer, Naomi, 36
Thayer, Noah, 33
Thayer, Olive, 44
Thayer, Oliver, 36, 74
Thayer, Olivia, 83
Thayer, Patience, 12
Thayer, Pelatiah, 97, 116, 117
Thayer, Perley, 44, 83
Thayer, Peter, 12, 36, 74
Thayer, Priscilla, 12, 35
Thayer, Rachel, 44, 45, 97, 116

Thayer, Rebecca, 44
Thayer, Reuben, 36, 73, 74
Thayer, Robert, 98
Thayer, Sabra, 44
Thayer, Samuel, 74
Thayer, Sarah, 6, 53
Thayer, Seth, 52
Thayer, Silas, 18, 44
Thayer, Silvanus, 36
Thayer, Simeon, 83
Thayer, Simon, 44
Thayer, Sophia, 87
Thayer, Sumner, 116, 128
Thayer, Sybil, 61
Thayer, Sybille, 87
Thayer, Sylvanus, 74
Thayer, Sylvia, 117
Thayer, Thankful, 72
Thayer, Thomas, 9, 11, 12
Thayer, Walter Grovenor, 117
Thayer, Walter J., 117
Thayer, William, 117
Thayer, William H., 45, 83, 129
Thomas Jefferson Darling, 89
Thomas, Freelove, 77
Thomas, Katherine, 94
Thomas, Lucy, 109
Thompson, Benjamin, 11
Thompson, Benoni, 11
Thompson, Comfort, 77
Thompson, Daniel, 19
Thompson, David, 19
Thompson, Ebenezer, 11
Thompson, Elisha, 19
Thompson, Elizabeth, 2, 11
Thompson, Gideon, 13
Thompson, Hannah, 14, 16
Thompson, Hezekiah, 19
Thompson, Jemima, 19, 48

Thompson, Joanna, 11
Thompson, John, 2, 9, 11, 12
Thompson, Lois, 42
Thompson, Lydia, 19
Thompson, Martha, 11
Thompson, Mary, 9, 11, 12, 19, 31, 41, 86
Thompson, Roger, 11
Thompson, Samuel, 11, 13
Thompson, Sarah, 5, 19
Thompson, Susanna, 19
Thompson, Susannah, 19
Thompson, Tamar, 11
Thompson, Timothy, 11
Thornton, Mehitable, 6
Throp, Mary, 14
Thwing, Almon, 65
Tillinghast, John, 15
Titus, Hannah, 30
Tower, Charlotte, 55
Tower, Joseph, 31
Tower, Lydia, 60
Town, Sally A., 44
Trask, Daniel, 10
Trask, Rachel, 35
Tucker, Rheuamy, 124
Turner, Chauncey, 126
Turner, Clarence Helmer, 132
Turner, Clarinda G., 126, 130
Turner, Elisha Skinner, 132
Turner, Ella, 126
Turner, Francis Helmer, 126
Turner, Helen Salisbury, 132
Turner, Jesse Smith, 126
Turner, John, 131
Turner, John Wallace, 132
Turner, Kate, 126
Turner, Mary, 84, 126
Turner, Olive Trowbridge, 132

Turner, Peter Halmer, 112, 126
Turner, Sarah, 126
Turner, William de Garmo, 131
Tyler, Patty, 50

U

Underwood, Charles, 57
Underwood, Joshua, 6

V

Vandevender, Mary, 74
Veazie, Amelia, 56
Vorce, Peggy, 72

W

Wade, Betsey, 92
Wade, William, 92
Walcott, Emeline Darling, 82
Walling, Arca, 56
Walling, Jacob, 83
Walling, Ruth, 83, 115
Ware, Eleazer, 15
Ware, Lydia, 15
Warfield, Elizabeth, 32
Warfield, Ithamar, 22
Warfield, Mary/Polly, 64
Warren, Mary, 42
Washburn, Lusina, 48
Washburn, Sarah, 24
Waterhouse, Jane, 116
Waterhouse, Sarah, 116
Webb, Charles Henry, 47
Webb, Daniel, 8
Webb, Margaret, 8
Webb, Walter, 89
Webber, Emma, 127
Weilbrecht, Herbert U., 125

Wells, Salome, 63
West, Anna, 13
Wheaton, Mary, 1
Wheelock, Abial, 32
Wheelock, Alexander, 21
Wheelock, Amariah, 22
Wheelock, Amoret, 52
Wheelock, Bathsheba, 21, 52
Wheelock, Benjamin, 6, 22, 29
Wheelock, Daniel, 22, 23, 29,
  49, 53
Wheelock, Deborah, 23
Wheelock, Ebenezer, 6
Wheelock, Eleazer, 21
Wheelock, Elias, 21, 51
Wheelock, Elizabeth, 6, 22
Wheelock, Experience, 21
Wheelock, Hannah, 6, 22, 23,
  49
Wheelock, Isabel, 22
Wheelock, Josiah, 6, 21
Wheelock, Levi, 22
Wheelock, Margaret, 6
Wheelock, Mary, 22, 23, 29,
  71
Wheelock, Obadiah, 5, 6, 21,
  22
Wheelock, Olive, 21
Wheelock, Paul, 22, 29, 52
Wheelock, Rachel, 22
Wheelock, Rebecca, 6
Wheelock, Rhoda, 23, 29
Wheelock, Rowena, 52, 88
Wheelock, Samuel, 6, 22
Wheelock, Sarah, 33
Wheelock, Thankful, 21
Wheelock, Zipporah, 73
Whetson, Ann, 65
Whipple, Amey, 60
Whipple, Dorcas, 77
Whipple, Eunice, 46

Whipple, Leonidas, 77
Whipple, Martha, 99
Whipple, Simon, 99
Whipple, Thankful, 98
Whitcomb, Mary, 54
White, Aaron, 53
White, Abigail, 73
White, Cynthia, 115
White, John, 20, 27, 32
White, Joseph, 28
White, Josiah, 73
White, Levi, 35, 36
White, Lydia, 5, 117
White, Mehitable, 6
White, Prudence, 53
White, Rachel, 20, 28
White, Sarah, 27
White, Thomas, 6
White, Trial, 73
Whitemere, Betsey, 68
Whiting, Ephraim, 31
Whiting, Jerusha, 36
Wight, Hannah, 9, 11, 12
Wight, Samuel, 11
Wilbur, Mary, 93, 108
Wilcox, Samuel, 105
Wilkinson, Amey, 25, 34
Wilkinson, Joanna, 61
Wilkinson, John, 25
Wilkinson, Jonathan, 25
Wilkinson, Lucy C., 79
Willard, Martha, 33
Williams, John, 21
Wilmarth, Benjamin, 31
Wilmarth, Hiram, 65
Wilson, Benjamin, 41, 80
Wilson, Eliza, 80, 106
Wilson, Israel, 41
Wilson, John, 4
Wilson, Joseph, 41
Wilson, Martha, 40

Wilson, Pintas, 27
Wilson, Robert, 41
Winch, Henrietta, 87
Winter, Hannah, 8
Witherbee, William A., 122
Wood, Howard, 46
Wood, Lydia, 57, 58
Wood, Mary, 48
Woodland, Thankful, 2

Woods, Molly, 68
Woodward, Julia Ann, 50

Y

Young, Levi, 64
Young, Polly, 64
Young, Rhoda, 51